*read*iscover...

BooksMusicFilmInformation**Computers**Local histor
Family history Newspapers **MagazinesPhotocopyin**
FaxingGamesChildren's storytimes Displays and event

Please return or renew this item by its due date to
avoid fines. It may be renewed by phone, online or
in person. Please quote the number on your library card.

Bletchley:	(01908) 372797
Kingston:	(01908) 282720
MK Central:	(01908) 254050
Newport Pagnell:	(01908) 610933
Olney:	(01234) 711474
Stony Stratford:	(01908) 562562
Westcroft:	(01908) 507874
Woburn Sands:	(01908) 582033
Wolverton:	(01908) 312812

www.milton-keynes.gov.uk/libraries

Milton Keynes **Libraries**

MILTON KEYNES
COUNCIL

79 324 980 7

By the same author

Animal Rights: A Christian Assessment

Animals and Ethics (Working Party Report)

Heaven and Earth: Essex Essays in Theology and Ethics (co-editor)

Christianity and the Rights of Animals

Research on Embryos: Politics, Theology and Law (co-author)

Theology, the University and the Modern World (co-editor)

Animals and Christianity: A Book of Readings (co-editor)

Compassion for Animals: Readings and Prayers (co-editor)

Song of Creation (co-editor)

Political Theory and Animal Rights (co-editor)

Prisoners of Hope (co-editor)

The Sayings of Jesus (editor)

Fundamentalism and Tolerance: An Agenda for Theology and Society (co-editor)

Cruelty and Christian Conscience (editor)

Animal Theology

Dictionary of Ethics, Theology and Society (co-editor)

After Noah: Animals and the Liberation of Theology (co-author)

Animals on the Agenda: Questions about Animals for Theology and Ethics (co-editor)

The Duty of Mercy and the Sin of Cruelty (editor)

Animal Rites: Liturgies of Animal Care

Animal Gospel

Andrew Linzey

Westminster John Knox Press
Louisville, Kentucky

Original edition published in Great Britain in 1998 under the title *Animal Gospel:
Christian Faith as if Animals Mattered* by Hodder & Stoughton.

The right of Andrew Linzey to be identified as the Author of the Work has been
asserted by him in accordance with the Copyright, Designs and Patents Act
1988.

Published in the United States in 2000
by WESTMINSTER JOHN KNOX PRESS
Louisville, Kentucky

Book design by Sharon Adams
Cover design by PAZ Design Group
Cover art PEACEABLE KINGDOM
            © 1969 John August Swanson
            Crayon sgraffito 14″ by 14″

Represented by the Bergsma Gallery, Grand Rapids, Michigan, (616) 458-1776.
John August Swanson paintings and limited-edition serigraphs are available
from this gallery.

Full-color posters and cards of Mr. Swanson's work are available from the National Association for Hispanic Elderly. Proceeds benefit its programs of em-
ployment and housing for low-income seniors. For information, contact
National Association of Hispanic Elderly, 234 East Colorado Blvd., Suite 300,
Pasadena, CA 91101, (626) 564-1988.

This book is printed on acid-free paper that meets the American National Standards Institute Z39.48 standard. ♾

PRINTED IN THE UNITED STATES OF AMERICA

00 01 02 03 04 05 06 07 08 09—10 9 8 7 6 5 4 3 2

Library of Congress Cataloging-in-Publication Data

Linzey, Andrew.
    Animal Gospel / Andrew Linzey.
        p.   cm.
    ISBN 0-664-22193-9 (alk. paper)
    1. Animal rights—Religious aspects—Christianity.   2. Animal welfare—Bib-
lical teaching.   3. Bible. N.T. Gospels—Criticism, interpretation, etc. I. Title.
BT746.L559 1999
241e'.693—dc21   99-33963
                                                                            CIP

For my daughter
Clair,
whose faith and sense of justice
has been an inspiration

Contents

Introduction: A Christian Credo for Animals

In this book I present my own vision of the Christian Gospel and how it can illuminate our understanding of our relationship with animals. This has necessitated a personal, confessional kind of book quite unlike any other I have written. I have wanted, however inadequately, to give some account of the faith that is within me—a faith which has inspired and encouraged me to work for more than a quarter of a century in defense of animals.

I have felt compelled to do this for four reasons. In the first place I believe with all my heart that the Christian Gospel is true. I say "with all my heart" because believing is about the heart as well as the head. Christian commitment is not and never has been just about mental assent. It is about having grasped—or rather having been grasped by—a kind of truth that requires a response of the heart, mind, and soul. My old college dean, Sydney Evans, used to speak of "the truth that is in Christ Jesus—for head, heart, and hand."[1] A response of all that we are, in other words, to the love of God revealed in Jesus Christ.

I want to give testimony that faith in this Gospel is the most precious thing in the world and that, without it, it is scarcely possible to have any human hope at all, yet alone sustain the daily struggle of living. For me the choice has always been between theism and nihilism. There is either reason to hope or nothing to hope for; good news or no news at all. Yet there are parts of me that do not want to believe, that constantly fear that the Gospel is too good to be true.

Because my own experience of doubt and despair has been so

extensive, I think I can understand those who feel that a life without ultimate hope is honestly better than a life with an apparent surfeit of belief. But I must confess what I know to be true, that such a life, however honest, is insufficient to energize moral endeavor or inspire realization of the highest human potential. We can live with nihilism—I myself have manifestly done so for periods of my life—but its inevitable result is a shrunken human life in which, to borrow words from John Clare:

> there is neither sense of life or joys,
> But the vast shipwreck of my life's esteems.[2]

Second, I believe that without faith in the Gospel we are inexorably led to a fundamental kind of despair about animal suffering. The truth is that nihilism renders not only our own lives morally void but also the whole world of suffering fellow creatures as well. It is not for nothing that those most adamant in their sense of the hopelessness of the world frequently cite the apparent futility of animal pain. As C. S. Lewis rightly discerns, "I know there are times when the incessant continuity and desperate helplessness of what seems at least to be animal suffering makes every argument for Theism appear hollow . . ."[3] But if the existence of animal pain is problematical for Christian faith (as it surely is), nihilism requires us neither to address it as a moral problem (how could it be a problem in a morally meaningless world?) nor indeed to do anything about it. Animal pain is a "problem" for Christian belief because its manifest futility is unreconcilable with the God of the Gospel.

Third, I believe that our indifference to animal suffering is a sign that we have not allowed the Gospel to speak to us. Baptist preacher Charles Spurgeon once recounted the view of Rowland Hill that a person "was not a true Christian if his dog or cat were not the better off for it," and commented, "That witness is true."[4] I think the matter can be put even more starkly: We have failed to see the face of the Crucified in the faces of suffering animals. We have not allowed the Gospel of Christ to interpret the world of innocent suffering, and so have helped to create the very climate in which the Gospel is dismissed as irrelevant to the messy and tragic world of suffering, both human and nonhuman.

This book is also about a struggle—a struggle, as I see it, against the blindness and indifference of Christians and the Churches to the sufferings of animals. It is about how those individuals and institutions who could have become the voice of God's weaker creatures have justified cruelty and oppression. The book speaks of my frustration, my pain, my sadness, but most of all my inner conviction that Christ-like discipleship is singularly tested in compassion to the Christ-like sufferings of the weakest of all.

Lastly, there is an urgent pastoral need underlying the writing of this book. I am only too well aware that there are many people who are encouraged in their despair about the world by the Church itself. Every year I receive hundreds of letters from people who are deeply troubled by the indifference of the churches to animal suffering. Many of these people are dedicated Christians who find their own sense of loyalty to the Church severely strained. The following is just one example:

> As a (barely surviving) member of the Church of England, I found it such a relief to hear a theologian arguing . . . on an issue that I find of such central concern, but which nearly all Christians view as of little importance. Man seems to have taken the central place in C of E worship, and the self-regarding, practical indifference of nearly all Christians to nonhuman suffering appalls me. The way we now treat animals seems to me to be so insulting to God, whose creation they are . . . I am proud to be among the Shorham protesters [against live exports]—I wish I could say I was as proud to be a member of the Church of England.

This is a voice which is seldom heard in the meetings and synods and corridors of the churches—let alone in their official pronouncements. Yet this voice is representative of an increasing groundswell of opinion—much greater than church leaders have begun to appreciate. In so many ways church hierarchies are still deeply unresponsive to, and unrepresentative of, ethically enlightened attitudes to animals.

This book, then, is written for these people who feel despairing about the Church and who desperately need to see beyond the Church to the Gospel which the Church itself has not infrequently obscured. Theirs is a voice that deserves to be heard, and not, as so often happens, marginalized, silenced, or ridiculed. At the same time, this book is also for Christians already committed to the Gospel who are prepared to be ethically challenged and to see the Gospel in a new light. Gospel Christians—of all people— should be open to new illumination. I offer this book to them in the hope that, despite its many inadequacies, they will at least agree that there is something Christ-like in the care for animals which the book espouses.

As an academic, I spend most of my time in the making of arguments and, more often, making arguments about arguments. I think this is a job worth doing, and part of me still hankers after the ideal of the disinterested pursuit of truth. There is a case for dispassion, holding questions at arm's length in order to see what the issues really are. Moreover, I believe that in purely rational, intellectual terms the case for animals is much, much stronger than is commonly supposed. Animal advocates have nothing to fear from, and all to gain by, the increase of rational discussion. I, for one, am confident that truth will win out in argument—at least eventually.

At the same time, impartiality can become not just a professional technique but a habit of mind, so that one can reach one's deathbed without actually ever having committed oneself to anyone or anything. I shall never forget hearing the politician Richard Crossman in debate when confronted by a student who insisted that the issue (in this case equality of educational opportunity) was "too difficult to decide since there are arguments on both sides," and therefore advocated abstention from voting. Crossman replied to devastating effect: "Abstain today, and you might abstain tomorrow. In fact, abstaining might become a habit of life, and you will end up dying having abstained on all the important issues in life." I frequently fear that the idea of neutrality favored by some academics is often a mask for noninvolvement as a matter of principle in controversial issues. Not without justification, George MacLeod once defined an academic as "someone who can hold a vital issue at arm's length for a lifetime."[5]

Rational argument is, of course, important and has its uses, but it has to begin somewhere. More precisely, it has to begin with something *given*. Argument without insight is vacuous. I like the line of Charles Péguy that "Everything begins in mysticism and ends in politics."[6] At the heart of the animal movement is a fundamental change of perception. That change can be described quite simply: It is a move away from the idea that animals are things, machines, commodities, resources, here for our use, or means-to-human-ends, to the idea that animals are God-given sentient beings with their own intrinsic value, dignity, and rights. This insight is fundamental to understanding the whole contemporary debate about animals, and I make no apology for repeating it again and again in the pages that follow.

I believe that this insight is basically a spiritual insight, nothing less than a discovery of what is integral to the confession of God as Creator. If the issue of animals arouses passion and debate, it is because what is at stake is the true status of animals as fellow creatures with us in God's world. In the same way that the Christian faith stands or falls by the truth of the Gospel, so the contemporary animal rights movement stands or falls by the truth of its most basic insight. As I have put it elsewhere, "This is a moral and spiritual discovery as objective and as important as any other fundamental discovery, whether it be the discovery of stars or planets or the discovery of the human psyche."[7]

I have sought to write an inspirational book, one that will inspire and empower and, most of all, touch the hearts and souls of its readers. *Animal Gospel* may be construed as a pastoral, evangelical sequel to *Animal Theology*, which was published by SCM Press in 1994 and which has happily found many readers throughout the world.[8] In order to do this, I have written new material and also revisited, reworked, and revised a range of previous writing, including lectures and addresses, which have stood the test of time and which others have judged to have some inspirational quality about them. Keen students of my work will notice the reappearance of key phrases, even some paragraphs, from previously published work. Again, I make no apology for this. If something is worth saying, it is sometimes worth saying more than once. I have, however, worked hard to

eliminate internal repetition and to ensure that—for all its in-
tended inspiration—a coherent, systematic argument is developed chapter by chapter.

Part 1 ("The Gospel for Every Creature") looks critically at the
way in which Christian teaching has neglected animals. It takes
central but sometimes overlooked theological ideas—God's love
for the world, the Fallen nature of creation, God's sovereign
rights as Creator, the Christ-like innocence of sentient creatures—and shows how they can inform a fresh Christian understanding of animals. Part 2 ("Disengaging from the Works of
Darkness") examines the variety of ways in which we treat animals today—especially in experimentation, genetic manipulation, cloning, and fur trapping—and argues that these practices
are, from the standpoint of the Gospel, simply unenlightened.
The final two chapters focus on how we can begin to liberate ourselves from the exploitation of animals and specifically how
churches can begin to assist in this process of spiritual transformation. Chapter 1 and 9 can be read as an overview of the argument of each part of the book.

As is well known, I hold the world's first post in Christian theology and animal welfare—the IFAW Senior Research Fellowship
at Mansfield College, Oxford. I am ever aware of this privilege and
am deeply grateful to IFAW (the International Fund for Animal
Welfare) for its foresight and generosity in funding this position.
It is much to IFAW's credit that it is prepared to fund independent academic work in the much neglected ethical and theological dimensions of this topic. It is important, however, that the
views expressed in this book are not taken as representative of
that organization, still less as in any way constituting its official
policy. I alone am responsible for the views expressed and, as is
clear throughout the book, its contents entirely reflect my personal convictions.

This work, like all my others, would not have been possible without the love and support of my family. My wife, Jo, and my children,
Adam, Clair, Rebecca, and Jacob, have had to carry the burden of
a husband and father frequently preoccupied elsewhere. Writing is
a solitary business, and this has been especially so with this book
since it has forced me to make some hard judgments on fellow

Christians, which in turn has necessitated no little heart- and soul-searching. I shall always treasure Rebecca's comment—when faced with a father absent in mind or body—that "Daddy is caring for the animals again." The common vulnerability and moral innocence of young children and animals, sometimes touched upon in the book, has frequently reminded me of the strong connection—both historically and morally—between animals' rights and children's rights. This common cause deserves a book in itself, and one day, God willing, I shall repay the debt and write it.[9] Special thanks, too, to Jo for typing and editing the innumerable versions of the manuscript with such forbearance.

Lest my confession be lost in, or obscured by, the many words that follow, let me state it now and as simply as possible:

I affirm the One Creator God from whom all existence flows. I celebrate the common origin of all life in God. I undertake to cherish and love all creatures whose life belongs to God and exists for God's glory.

I affirm the life of Jesus as the true pattern of service to the weak. I promise my solidarity with all suffering creatures. I join hands with Jesus in his ministry to the least of all, knowing that it is the vocation of the strong to be gentle.

I see in the face of the Crucified the faces of all innocent, suffering creatures. I hear their cries for a new creation. I thank God for the grace to feel their suffering and give voice to their pain.

I affirm the Word made flesh as the new covenant between God and all sentient creatures. I seek to live out that covenant in acts of moral generosity, kindness and gentleness to all those creatures that God has gathered together into unity.

I affirm the life-giving Spirit, source of all that is wonderful, who animates every creature. I pledge myself to honor life because of the Lord of life.

I affirm the hope of the world to come for all God's creatures. I believe in the Cross as the symbol of liberation for every creature suffering from bondage. I will daily trust in the redeeming power of God to transform the universe.

I pray that the community of Christ may be blessed with a new vision of God's creation. I will turn away from my hardness of heart and seek to become a living sign of the Gospel for which all creatures long.

I rejoice in animals as fellow-creatures: loved by the Father, redeemed by the Son, and enlivened by the Holy Spirit.

May God the Holy Trinity give me strength to live out my commitment this day.[10]

Andrew Linzey
Mansfield College, Oxford

Part 1

The Gospel for Every Creature

1

Overview: Gospel Truths about Animals

I believe that the Gospel is at stake in the way we understand and treat animals. Believing the Gospel can, and should, make a *difference* to our daily interactions with other creatures. In this chapter, I give a personal account of the Gospel truths that have sustained my commitment to the cause of animals for more than twenty-five years.

So, why do I look to Jesus? When so many others look elsewhere, why is it that I find him an inspiration for animal rights work? Why not Darwin and the story of evolution? Or Albert Schweitzer and his notion of an ever-widening reverence for life? Or, indeed, St. Francis of Assisi and his claim that animals are our brothers and sisters? When so many others, both Christian and non-Christian, fail to see the connection, what moves me to confess Christ as an inspiration—in fact, *the* inspiration—for a revolutionary reappraisal of the status of animals?

I have no choice but to confess my faith, to give some account of what it is that moves me, inspires me, and creates in me a kind of inner conviction that to stand with Jesus means to stand against the abuse of animals. Here are my five articles of faith.

First, to stand for Jesus is to stand for animals as God's creatures, against all purely humanistic or utilitarian accounts of animals as things, commodities, resources, here for us. Sometimes I think that the most important contribution the Gospel can make to our thinking about the world is the simple assertion that we are not God. In the words I have often quoted from Hans von Balthasar: "The whole point of creation is for us to know that we are not Creator." To affirm that animals are creatures like us is to reject once and for all the deification of our kind that so characterizes humanistic perspectives on our prerogatives with regard to other species.

Far too often, Christians have accepted the common secular view that we are the masters of animals, their rulers or owners—utterly forgetting that the dominion promised to humanity is a deputized dominion, in which we are to stand before creation as God's vice-regents, putting into effect not our own egotistical wants but God's own law of love and mercy.[1] And yet, when one begins to challenge our despotic treatment of animals—whether killing for sport, the ruthless export trade, or (to take the latest example) the quite obscene slaughter of thousands of seals for their penises, to be sold as aphrodisiacs in Europe and Asia—again and again, one has to face this humanistic dogma: If it benefits humanity, it must be right.

Such thinking—and there is no getting away from it, Christians have also thought this way—betrays a fundamental spiritual impoverishment. For if animals are God's creatures, we have no absolute rights over them, only the duty to look after them as God would look after them. To stand with Jesus is to reject our view of ourselves as gods and lords of creation. We are to honor life for the sake of the Lord of life.

Second, to stand for Jesus is to stand for active compassion for the weak, against the principle that might is right. And I do not mean the kind of lukewarm geniality that often passes for compassion, but rather that full-blooded thing that is a biblical sign of moral regeneration. According to Colossians, Christians have discarded "the old nature with its deeds, and have put on the new nature, which is being constantly renewed [by Christ] in the image of its Creator." And we are enjoined to "put on the garments that suit God's chosen people, his own and beloved: compassion, kindness, humility, gentleness, patience."[2] These are Gospel garments for Gospel people.

With these thoughts in mind, we shall not ridicule, or even dare to smile at, those who feel the sufferings of God's creatures whether they be humans or animals. The Gospel truth is that we are empowered by divine grace to feel the suffering of others; that we can so feel is the accomplishment of Christ within us. It is nothing less than shocking to hear Christians speaking derisively of those who care for animals as "sentimentalists." What would these people have said of Jesus' compassion for all those beyond the normal boundaries of concern in his own day—the poor, the diseased, the marginalized, even tax collectors and prostitutes? Well, we know what they said: One of the rebukes from religious people was precisely this, that he made friends with them.[3] To be united to Christ involves in our own day an expansion of moral sensitivity no less an affront or a threat to those in power than was Jesus' own compassion in his day.

Indeed, there is something profoundly ignorant as well as shocking about the charge of sentimentality when it comes from evangelicals. For the modern evangelical founders of social reform—Lord Shaftesbury and William Wilberforce, to take only two examples—often regarded the cultivation of Christian sensibility as a precursor to moral progress.

Shaftesbury provided the rationale for the protection of animals that has guided Christians for well over a century: "I was convinced that God had called me to devote whatever advantages He might have bestowed upon me to the cause of the weak, the helpless, both man and beast, and those who had none to help them . . . Whatever I have done I was enabled to do; and all happy results (if any there be) must be credited, not to the servant, but to the great Master, who led and sustained him."[4]

Among his many achievements, with Cardinal Manning Shaftesbury co-founded the Victoria Street Society, the first in the world to campaign against vivisection. So great was his influence that after his death Frances Power Cobbe wrote: "Lord Shaftesbury never joined the Victoria Street Society; it was the society which joined Lord Shaftesbury."[5]

Third, to stand for Jesus is to stand for the Christ-like innocence of animals, against the intrinsic evil of cruelty. We have lived so long with the gospel stories of Jesus that we often fail to see how his life and ministry identified with animals. He was born in the home of sheep and oxen. His ministry began in the wilderness "with the wild beasts."[6] His triumphal entry into Jerusalem was on the back of a beast of burden.[7]

13

According to Jesus (at least by implication), it is lawful to "do good" on the Sabbath, which includes the rescuing of an animal fallen into a pit.[8] Even the sparrows, literally sold for a few pennies in his day, are "not forgotten by God." God's providence extends to the entire created order, and the glory of Solomon and all his works cannot be compared to that of the lilies of the field.[9] God so cares for creation that even "foxes have holes, and the birds of the air have nests," though "the Son of Man has nowhere to lay his head."[10]

But the most significant identification is that of Christ as "the Lamb of God."[11] As Cardinal Newman noted in a sermon in 1842, Scripture compares Christ to a humble and unprotected animal. Exploring this metaphor, Newman went on to posit the Christ-like innocence of animals and argued that cruelty to all innocents—whether they be children or animals—is morally equivalent to the cruelty inflicted on Christ himself.

Animal suffering represents nothing less than the innocent, undeserved suffering of Christ. Only Christians, whose eyes are focused on the awfulness of crucifixion, should be in a position to understand the awfulness of innocent suffering. Such suffering, whether it is of weaker members of the human community or of animals, calls to heaven for judgment and redemption. The Cross of Christ embraces the suffering of the whole creation; our sensitivity to that suffering is a litmus test of Christian discipleship. I would suggest that no theology that desensitizes us to suffering can possibly be Christian theology.

Fourth, to stand for Jesus is to stand for a ministry of reconciliation to the whole of creation, against the powers of darkness represented, at least in part, by the destructiveness of human technology. "For in him," writes Paul, "the complete being of God, by God's own choice, came to dwell. Through him God chose to reconcile the whole universe to himself, making peace through the shedding of his blood upon the cross—to reconcile all things, whether on earth or in heaven, through him alone."[12]

In the past, Christians have not been much exercised by the question of how they can share this ministry of reconciliation, and especially what it might mean to do so in this cosmic context. But one thing is clear: What is accomplished on the Cross has cosmic significance. Colossians and Ephesians cannot be read as affirmations of a purely humanocentric theology. We are invited to consider the ways in which creation is not yet reconciled to God.

Here, we reach another parting of the ways between Christians and non-Christians. For the latter, there is no Fall, either of humans or of anything else. The world is simply "as it is," and we must be reconciled to it as it is. But the Gospel truth is that we do not have to accept the world as it is. We must distinguish creation from nature. The world of nature is as yet unfinished. This means in practice that Christians cannot simply deduce from the world as it is what it will, or rather should, be.

This point is absolutely fundamental because those who want to exploit animals (Christians, regrettably, as well as secularists) are disposed to view the world as a moral textbook, so that humans are entitled to imitate whatever relationships of subordination, wantonness, or parasitism they may find there. The Gospel truth, however, is that the story of Jesus is not the story of Christ our Predator. The world of predation and all the suffering and death which accompany it stand against the Gospel of God's love.

Christians entrusted with a ministry of reconciliation to the whole of creation need to become credible signs of the Gospel for which all creatures long. This means that, however unreconciled nature may be, Christians cannot simply appeal to the "old nature" to justify present exploitation; indeed, the exact opposite is true. We must take on the powers in the world which exploit and degrade God's creatures—especially our own technological power which reduces animals to commodities and things.

The automated, institutionalized, routine destruction of billions of creatures every year, for food, for profit, for science and for sport, raises the question whether Christians have lost their grasp of the reality of evil. Animal rights constitute a spiritual struggle against the forces of cruelty and death.

Finally, to stand for Jesus is to stand for God's justice and the final release of all creation from bondage to decay, against the moral hopelessness and despair that characterize our time.

Whatever the "autonomy of ethics" means, I do not believe in it. Ethics cannot be divorced from theological vision. Without such vision, ethics perish. In the ecological crises of our day, we humans are learning this lesson the hard way, and with incalculable consequences (in terms of suffering alone) for the nonhuman world. To believe in Jesus is to believe that the cosmos is loved and blessed by God. It is not perfect, but it is going somewhere: It is in the process of being reconciled and will ultimately be redeemed. The whole creation groans and suffers, awaiting the revelation of the children of God who will help to release it from its bondage and futility.[13]

In my view, there is no more Christ-like work than the releasing of creation from this bondage, "for in this hope we are saved." To stand for Jesus is to stand within the purposes of God, which encompass far more than the salvation of humankind, vital though that is, and not just for humanity.

When the divine image, though marred by human sinfulness and violence, is renewed through Christ, there are new possibilities for all creation. The work of caring for creation, of saving animals from our own ruthlessness and greed, is an evangelical work, in that it shows forth the Gospel. This Gospel is about the faithfulness and justice of God who, despite all appearances, will not let us—or creation—down. Because of this, we need more, much more, "sentimentality" toward animals. Their plight is inextricably related to our full humanization in Christ.

To speak in this way nowadays strains credulity. Frankly, many Christians have given up on the Gospel idea of the redemption of all creation. The very most they are able to imagine is a saved and perfected humankind; the rest of nature (as it is) is the best we can envisage it to be. To parody this position a little (but only a little), the redeeming work of Christ can cope only with the human species. After all, they say, only half-joking, heaven would have to be a big place to hold all these animals as well.

But the real issue is not whether our picture of heaven is big enough but whether our vision of God is. The truth is that a new heaven and earth that cannot encompass redemption for each and every suffering creature is not big enough for the God of justice in whom Christians believe. If, as Michael Ramsey once put it, "God is Christ-like, and in him is no un-Christ-likeness at all,"[14] it is inconceivable that God the Father could be less compassionate than the Son.

Recently, the editor of the *Expository Times* accused me of "a failure to face up to the realities of the natural world."[15] Foolishly, I took this to be a compliment, until a colleague suggested otherwise. Failing to face up to—or rather, be circumscribed by—the realities of this world seems to me to be the necessary starting point of Christian ethics.

Christian ethics is essentially eschatological: It points us beyond this world to another. What my critic meant, of course, was not that I would not face the realities of this world but that I would not share *his perception* of what is God-given (and so unalterable) in the present world. Our belief in God is so often tied to a way of viewing the world which sets preconceived limits to what God can actually do with it.

As with "nature," so with "human nature": We all have our limits and suppose that God cannot, or will not, operate beyond them. The biblical doctrine of the redemption of creation strikes at the root of our timid conceptions of God's providence. The God of Isaac, of Jacob, of Abraham, and of Jesus is not limited by what we know of elementary biology. If what is revealed in Jesus is eternally true of the nature of God, then it must be the same hand that heals lepers which also transforms the whole suffering cosmos. In short, those who say God cannot redeem the world sell Jesus short.

The question "Who do we think we are in creation?" is theologically urgent. If only Christians and churches could regain a new kind of confidence in their own Gospel theology, we might be able to show our contemporaries a vision of how creation should be and a corresponding sense of moral limits. Karl Barth wrote, "Tell me how it stands with your Christology, and I shall tell you who you are."[16] It may be that what we believe about Christ is far more significant for the future of God's other creatures than we could possibly imagine.

2

For God So Loved the World

Christians frequently talk about God as the loving Creator of all things. Indeed one of the earliest things said about Christians—as their defining characteristic—was "how they love one another." But Christian love, even if it begins with loving our immediate neighbors, should not end there. For the God of Jesus Christ is an inclusive lover, not just of Christians or human beings but all creatures. Recapturing this vision of God as lover of all creation is essential to grasping the Gospel and its implications for our treatment of animals. In this chapter, I give an account of this inclusive vision of Christian loving and the challenge it represents both to the churches and animal advocates alike.

Imagine a scene. The date is April 18, 1499. The time is sometime in the afternoon. The place is the Abbey of Josaphat, near Chartres. Within this abbey a trial is taking place. It is a criminal prosecution before the Bailiff of the Abbey. The defendant is charged with having killed an infant. The verdict is announced. The defendant is found guilty. The sentence of the ecclesiastical court is that the defendant should be hanged. Mercifully, unlike for other defendants, the fate is only death and not torture or mangulation. And the defendant was hanged by its neck at a public hanging that day in the market square. The defendant, however, was not a human being, but a pig.[1]

What is the point of recounting this grisly, surely altogether extraordinary episode from the fifteenth century, you may ask? The answer is this: Grisly it certainly was; extraordinary it certainly was not. From the ninth to the nineteenth century we have innumerable written accounts of the criminal prosecution and capital punishment of animals. These trials of animals, pigs, dogs, wolves, locusts, rats, termites, cows, horses, and doves inflicted great and terrible suffering. And the important thing to appreciate is that these trials were mainly or wholly religious in character. They drew their inspiration from Christian teaching. In particular it was St. Thomas Aquinas in his *Summa Theologiae* who held that some animals were satellites of Satan, "instigated by the powers of hell and proper to be cursed." St. Thomas added, "The anathema then is not to be pronounced against the animals as such, but should be hurled inferentially at the devil who makes use of irrational creatures to our detriment."[2]

Armed with this awful dictum (however originally qualified by St. Thomas), Christians have spent more than ten centuries anathematizing, cursing, and reviling the animal world. The echoes of this violence are found today in our very language. The word "animal" is a term of abuse, not to mention "brute," "beast," or "bestial." How we have libeled the animal world! For myself I cannot but be bemused by the reference in the marriage service of *The Book of Common Prayer* to "brute beasts which hath no understanding." Who are these brute beasts? Many higher mammals seem to know more about lifelong monogamy than many human beings.

This low, negative, even hating, attitude toward animals, regarding them as a source of evil or as instruments of the devil, or regarding them as beings without any moral status, has, sad to say, been the dominant view within Christendom for the largest part of its history. In the ninth century, Pope Stephen IV prepared great quantities of holy water with which to anathematize hordes of locusts. In the nineteenth century, Pope Pius IX forbade the opening of an animal protection office in Rome on the grounds that humans had duties to other humans but none to animals. For a clear run of at least ten centuries, the dominant ecclesiastical voice did not even regard animals as worthy of moral concern. We do well to remember that Catholic textbooks until very recently still regarded humans as having no direct duties to animals, only duties *concerning* them, when, for example, they are deemed human property.[3] Moreover, they have been frequently classified as things without rights, to be used—as St. Thomas himself wrote—"either by killing or in any other way whatever."[4] If Jesus can weep over Jerusalem, we have more than good reason to weep over the sins of Mother Church.

It seems to me that there is no use pretending that all has been well with the Church, either in the past or even now in the present. The very community which should be the cradle of the Gospel of God's love for the world has been only too good at justifying violence and legitimizing hatred toward the world. Those like me who have the temerity to preach to Christian and non-Christian alike must be quite clear that the record of Christianity has been, and still is, on this issue as on many others, in many respects shameful and second-rate. Christians are simply too good at forgetting how awful they have been. The fact is that Christians have had enormous difficulties in believing their own Gospel.

And what is this Gospel? It is nothing less than the conviction and experience that God loves the whole world. What we see in Jesus is the revelation of an inclusive, all-embracing, generous loving. A loving that washes the feet of the world. A loving that heals individuals from oppression, both physical and spiritual. A loving that takes sides with the poor, vulnerable, diseased, hated, despised, and outcasts of his day. A loving that is summed up in his absolute commitment to love at all costs, even in extreme suffering and death. As Sydney Evans once wrote, "What Jesus did on the Cross was to demonstrate the truth of what he had taught: he showed a quality of love—such that the worst that evil could do to such love was to give such love ever fresh opportunities for loving."[5]

The world we live in is desperate for love. The whole world needs to be loved. When I was young I used to mock the notion of "Gentle Jesus, meek and mild." How wrong I was! For there is great power in humility, strength in gentleness, wisdom in forbearance. We need to listen again to Father Zossima's advice in Dostoevsky's *The Brothers Karamazov*:

> Brothers, be not afraid of men's sins. Love man even in
> his sin, for that already bears the semblance of divine

love and is the highest love on earth. Love all God's creation, the whole of it and every grain of sand. Love every leaf, every ray of God's light! Love the animals, love the plants, love everything. And if you love everything you will perceive the divine mystery in things. And once you have perceived it, you will begin to comprehend it ceaselessly more and more every day. And you will at last come to love the whole world with an abiding, universal love.[6]

Not all Christians have been happy with this Gospel. While God's love is free, generous, and unlimited, Christians have been only too good at placing limits on Divine Love. St. Thomas Aquinas was a great scholar and saint, but even he believed, quite erroneously, that God did not love animals for their own sakes, but only in so far as they were of use to human beings. Christians have at various times made of this Revelation of Unlimited Love its precise opposite. We have conceived of this Revelation in exclusive terms, exclusive to one group or race: those who are non-Jews, those who are women, those of a different ethnic background, and so on. Not all Christians have seen how the love of God gives each individual human being a unique and equal value. But at least we can say that these issues have been on the agenda of the churches. Not so with other suffering nonhuman creatures. What has not been seen is that the love of God is inclusive not only of humans *but also all creatures*. It took Christians many years to realize that we cannot love God and also keep humans as slaves. It has taken even longer for Christians to realize that we cannot love God and also regard women as second-class humans. Now is the time for Christians to realize that we cannot love God and hate the Creator's nonhuman creatures. Christians are people who need to be liberated by the Gospel they preach. Christians cannot both love God and be free to hate.

For people like me, who are concerned for justice in our dealings with animals, there are three things we must learn.

The first is that we must not hate even those who hate animals. "Do not be afraid of men's sins," writes Dostoevsky. People who work for justice for animals are often disappointed, angry, unhappy people, and more often than not with just cause.

It is incredible that we should treat God's creatures with so little love and respect; incredible that we should despoil animal life for fun and amusement; incredible that we should wantonly slaughter; incredible that we should make wild animals captive for entertainment; incredible that we should inflict suffering and pain on farm and laboratory animals. It is spiritually infantile that we should continue to look upon the world as "made for us" and animals simply as means to human ends, as resources, as tools, as machines, indeed simply as things. And yet we must not hate those who hate God's world. By doing so we simply push them further into their own abyss and spiritual darkness. All of us need to be loved; all of us need interior resources to go on loving. And all this is very, very hard, especially when we see creatures treated so cruelly that their cause cries to heaven for justice. But we have one real and lasting weapon at our disposal: "Soul force." As Dostoevsky writes, "Loving humility is a terrible force, the strongest of all, and there is nothing like it."[7]

So I don't want to hate anybody, even vivisectors, butchers, trappers, factory farmers, and bullfighters. On the contrary, I want to love them so much that they will not find time, or have the inclination, to hunt, and kill, and destroy and maim God's good creatures. I refuse to give those who exploit animals another good reason for not believing in a God of love.

Second, we must not hate even the Church. I know that this is very difficult, not least of all because the Church has a lamentable record on animals and, what is more, is still a party to animal cruelty. Christians must be signs of the Gospel for which all creatures long. I know that the Church is not always very lovable to say the least. But we shall not advance the cause of animals by hating the Church. On the contrary, we must love it so much that it repents of its theological foolishness, its far too frequent humanist arrogance and its complicity in sins against animals. In the words of Martin Luther King: "I've seen too much hate to want to hate . . . and every time I see it, I say to myself hate is too great a burden to bear."[8]

I want to give you one example that should give us hope. If we go back two hundred years or so, we will find intelligent, respectable, conscientious Christians for whom slavery was not a moral issue. If pressed some might have defended slavery as "progress," as many thought it was. The quite staggering fact to grapple with is that this very same community, which in some ways provided the major ideological impetus for the defense of slavery, came, within an historically short period—one hundred, perhaps only fifty years—to change its mind. The same tradition which helped keep slavery alive was the same community that became by and large determined to end it. So successful has this change been that today we would have difficulty in finding one slave trader, even one individual Christian, who thinks that the practice is anything other than inimical to the moral demands of the Christian faith. In short, while it is true that Christian churches have been and frequently are awful on the subject of animals, it is just possible, even plausible that given, say, fifty or a hundred years, we should witness among this same community amazing shifts of consciousness as we have witnessed them on other moral issues no less complex or controversial. Christian churches have then been agents of oppression—that is commonplace—but they can also be agents of liberation.[9]

We do well in this context to remember and honor all those courageous Christians: saints and seers, theologians and poets, mystics and writers who have championed the cause of animals. The list must include almost two-thirds of those canonized saints East and West, not only St. Francis but also St. Martin, Richard of Chichester, Chrysostom, Isaac the Syrian, Bonaventure, and countless others. The list must also include poets like Rosetti, Browning, Carlyle, Longfellow, Hardy, and Cowper who have pioneered sensitivity to the animal world.[10] The books have yet to be written that properly recognize and celebrate their contribution to the cause of animal protection. At its best, the Christian tradition has been a powerhouse for humanitarian feeling and yet—when it comes to animals—we have failed even to recognize our humanitarian pioneers.

The third thing we must learn is that we must not hate one another. People like me in the animal rights movement complain about animal abusers and the churches for their lack of love and compassion, but who will listen when we so often show so little love and compassion to one another? I can give personal testimony here. I spent four years on the ruling council of one of the largest animal welfare societies in England, and twenty or more years later I am still trying to heal the wounds I suffered. The animal movement is a place where we can find as much if not more sin as anywhere else: jealousy, rivalry, misquotation, guile, stupidity, and, worst of all, self-righteousness. We must not fall into this last trap especially. None of us is pure when it comes to animals. There is no pure land on earth. A clean conscience is a figment of the imagination. I used to spend a lot of my time as a university chaplain counseling students who suffered from unrelieved feelings of guilt, often inculcated by the churches. I have no desire to make anyone feel guilty. Guilt—unlike shame—is a redundant emotion.

Christians in the animal movement have a unique opportunity. St. Paul speaks of the creation as in a state of childbirth awaiting a new age. Together we have a vision of a new age, a new world: a world at peace, a world in which we have begun to make peace with creation, a world in which the love of God is claimed and championed and through whose Spirit new world possibilities are constantly being opened up for us. What a difference it would make if Christians began to practice the Gospel of Love they preach.

When I became intellectually convinced of the case for animal rights, I first thought it one of those important but comparatively minor questions in Christian ethics. I don't think that today. On the contrary, I think the question of how we treat animals is one of the *big* questions confronting all humanity: If God loves and cares for this world, shall we learn to live at peace with one another and with this world? In short, are we to hate the world or are we to love it? "We must love one another or die," wrote W. H. Auden.[11] Perhaps the corollary truth we also have to learn is this: We must love the world, or we shall perish with it.

3

Unfinished
and Unredeemed
Creation

Even among biblical and evangelical Christians, the idea of the Fall of creation has increasingly lost favor, being now frequently regarded as one of those items of traditional belief that can be lost or jettisoned without harming central doctrines like creation and incarnation. In this chapter I try to show why this idea of the Fall is altogether more central and important than its detractors allow. Most especially, I try to bring out the moral and theological consequences of such a rejection for our understanding of animal life. I begin with a story:

> [Philip, Bartholomew and Mariamne] all set out [as directed by the Lord] for the land of Ophiani; and when they came to the wilderness of dragons, behold, a great leopard came out of a wood on the hill, and ran and cast himself at their feet and spoke with human voices, "I worship you servants of the divine greatness and apostles of the only-begotten Son of God; command me to speak perfectly." And Philip said, "In the name of Jesus Christ, speak." And the leopard adopted perfect speech and said, "Hear me Philip, groomsman of the divine word. Last night I passed through the flocks of goats near the mount of the she-dragon, the mother of snakes, and seized a kid; and when I went into the wood to eat, after I had wounded it, it took a human voice and wept like a little child, saying to me, 'O leopard, put off your fierce heart and the beastlike part of your nature, and put on mildness, for the apostles of the divine greatness are about to

pass through this desert, to accomplish perfectly the promise of the glory of the only-begotten Son of God.' At these words of the kid I was perplexed, and gradually my heart was changed, and my fierceness turned into mildness, and I did not eat it. And as I listened to its words, I lifted up my eyes and saw you coming, and knew that you were servants of the good God. So I left the kid and came to worship you. And now I beseech you to give me liberty to go with you everywhere and put off my beastlike nature."

And Philip said, "Where is the kid?" And he said, "It is cast down under the oak opposite." Philip said to Bartholomew, "Let us go and see him that was smitten, healed, and healing the smiter." And at Philip's bidding the leopard guided them to where the kid lay. Philip and Bartholomew said, "Now know we of a truth that there is none that surpasses your compassion, O Jesu, lover of man; for you protect us and convince us by these creatures to believe more and earnestly fulfil our trust. Now, therefore, Lord Jesus Christ, come and grant life and breath and secure existence to these creatures, that they may forsake their nature of beast and cattle and come unto tameness, and no longer eat flesh, nor the kid the food of cattle; but that men's hearts may be given them, and they may follow us wherever we go, and eat what we eat, to your glory, and speak after the manner of men, glorifying your name."

And in that hour the leopard and the kid rose up and lifted up their forefeet and said, "We glorify and bless you who have visited and remembered us in this desert, and changed our beastlike and wild nature into tameness, and granted us the divine word, and put in us a tongue and sense to speak and praise your name, for great is your glory." And they fell and worshipped Philip and Bartholomew and Mariamne; and all set out together, praising God.[1]

The story is taken from *The Acts of Philip*, one of five principal apostolic romances written in the fourth and fifth centuries. It forms part of a quite voluminous quantity of non-canonical material whose origins and dating are frequently obscure. One of the recurring themes of this literature concerns the establishing or restoration of peaceful and friendly relationships with animals.

I have deliberately chosen this story because it is fantastic—so fantastic that some may not be surprised to learn that it was never included in any recognizable canon of scripture and is described by the editor himself as "edifying fiction."[2] It is fantastic too in another more important sense: It makes the strongest possible claim on our imagination. Rachel Trickett has wryly observed how theologians are "peculiarly reluctant to concede the innate human capacity to accept the marvelous, to delight in wonder and respond to the strongest claims on the imagination." She explains, "Artists, by contrast, always assume it; the justification of their work depends upon it."[3]

I foray into this little discussion about imagination, belief, and truth because so much in the Christian tradition, like the work of a good artist, makes the strongest possible claim on our imagination. Partly because so much in the tradition strikes us as "imaginary," we are inclined to reject it. But, as Trickett observes, such a rejection, if pursued to its logical conclusion, would lead us to the rejection of almost all literature and the moral insight which results from it.

Trickett defines the problem in this way: ". . . the act of consenting or believing, like any act of the will, involves that quality of imagination which can entertain and hold in the mind the completeness of a complex truth with all its many facets." She defines the role of imagination as follows: "To see truth as a process of stripping bare, paring away, is a common rational perception; to see truth as a gathering together, a process of accretion which may appear to lead to paradox and contradiction, but which, in the end, resolves them by asserting completeness, is a function of the imagination."[4]

What is at stake in the question of the Fall is nothing less than our imagination, that faculty which can help us—in Trickett's words—to hold "in the mind the completeness of a complex truth," and at the same time our fidelity or—more often than not—infidelity to the moral insights to which it gives rise. In theological terms the complex truth to which this debate corresponds is the dual recognition that God as the Creator of all

27

things must have created a world which is morally good—or at least be justified in the end as a morally justifiable process—and also the insight that parasitism and predation are unlovely, cruel, evil aspects of the world ultimately incapable of being reconciled with a God of love.

The concept of the Fall—whether it be deduced from Genesis, or by implication from Romans 8 or Isaiah 11, or from the narrative in Philip, or indeed from the countless stories of the saints who befriend animals and save them from predator/prey relations—constitutes a composite rejection of the idea that the creation as it is now is, at least in this respect, God's original will. Such an insight resulting from "holding together in the mind a complex truth" is as fundamentally important to Christian theology as any doctrinally formulated belief whether of Chalcedon or Nicea. To reject it, as many theologians do today, simply on the grounds that it is an imaginative story, or as incidentally the editor of Philip did by suggesting that it could not be as important as other material because it was more interested in "narrative" than "doctrine," is perverse.[5] The truth is that theologians are even more adept than nonbelievers in seeing truth as a "paring away" rather than as a "gathering together," but in the process of doing so they fail to see that they make theology not less incredible but more so. The very faculty which, humanly speaking, provides integrity for the whole system is cut away, and theologians spend their time debating which little bits of the system may be rendered intelligible after the central stories have been disregarded.

Therefore, it seems vital to spell out as precisely as possible what kind of inchoate theology will be left if those who wish to reject the notion of the Fall have their way. To reject the fallenness of creation means that:

1. *There is no evil in the natural world.* Predation and parasitism are either morally neutral or, even worse, positive aspects of nature to be tolerated or even emulated. Quite practically lions disembowelling gazelles, cuckoos pushing non-cuckoos out of the nest, tarantulas eating their prey, are not, *cannot be*, moral matters. They

may be matters of taste, hygiene, or aesthetics, but they cannot be moral ones. To deny the Fall is to live within a nature that is divorced from ethical truth. The moral realm no longer includes the nonhuman. "Human morality"—and it is often so called—has no relevance to the natural realm except possibly insofar as it adversely affects us, and then only indirectly as a moral problem. To be appalled, shocked, outraged by the apparent senselessness and futility of nature is a category mistake like being appalled by washing or eating or sexual relations—all prima facie without a moral dimension.

2. *There is no possibility of redemption for nature, animals in particular.* Instead the cruelty and awfulness of nature become, in theological terms, agents of a now morally compromised God. Richard Cartwright Austin goes so far as to extol the "beauty" of predation when witnessing a fish eagle taking its prey.[6] God must now abide by a new law of the universe, as Matthew Fox puts it: "Eat and get eaten."[7] Gone is the operation of the Holy Spirit within creation leading to its rescue from bondage to decay. Absent is the whole eschatological frame of reference, so central to early Christian reflection upon nature, that creation can only properly be interpreted from the standpoint of its eventual consummation.[8] Nature cannot be redeemed because there is nothing to be improved upon—no evil to be overcome, no pain to be healed, and no new heaven and earth for which all creatures long. This view deserves the admonition of Luther who, in exegesis of Romans 8, argued: "We conclude, therefore, that anyone who searches into the essences and functionings of the creatures rather than into their sighings and earnest expectations is certainly foolish and blind. He does not know that also the creatures are created for an end."[9] Whatever the limitations of Luther's theology of animals, he grasped here that a redeeming God could not eschew the sighing and suffering of all creatures.

3. *There is no human obligation to cooperate with God in the redemption of nature, animals in particular.* If the awfulness of

animal suffering in nature is morally neutral, even divine will, there can be no summons to alleviate that evil or to regard as a Christian-like task the healing of disordered relationships within creation. Quite simply, the human task does not and cannot include the natural world. "Human morality" is properly for humans only—except perhaps in this one regard: eat and be eaten. It is astonishing that ecologists should so readily have taken up this neo-Darwinian slogan with such unfortunate implications for human as well as natural society. For if God, the Lord and Sustainer of all that is, is so logically determined by this one inexorable law of the universe, shall we be so naive as to suppose that such a limited God is actually interested in a wholly different, indeed contradictory, norm for human society? However unsophisticated the general theological view of Philip in his narrative of the leopard and the kid, he preserves for us the insight that the Gospel of Jesus has implications for the life of each and every sentient being. Whether or not a neo-Darwinian version of divine limitation can sustain human life from the very same predation which it sees as the inexorable law of the universe in relation to nature and animals seems highly questionable. The idea that we begin by being insensitive to animals and then proceed to a similar insensitivity to humans may not be as ideologically ungrounded as some had supposed.

4. *There is no morally just God.* This of course is the inevitable conclusion, already implicit in the work of some of the anti-Fall theologians, to which their whole argument points. God cannot be God to nature in at least this one crucially determining respect: God cannot redeem nature. But if this is true, then it must also be true that God is a morally capricious being whose purpose or plan in creating is morally flawed and to which we humans hold no duty of allegiance and certainly not worship. It is really important to get this matter straight: We may from time to time entertain genuine doubts and difficulties in relation to what may be God's purpose in creation and how that purpose

may eventually be achieved; we may even have doubts about the means and the ends implicit in such a process; we may be especially doubtful about how far human activity can directly or indirectly contribute to the divinely purposed new heaven and earth; but however admissible, legitimate, even compelling these doubts may be, to reject absolutely the possibility of a transformed new heaven and earth in which all sentients will be redeemed is logically tantamount to denying the possibility of a morally good God. A nonredeeming God in relation to nature is worse than a no-God; it is to endorse the common despair that all life is morally hopeless because there is no moral justifiability for its existence.

I have stated these implications (as I see them) boldly and provocatively because great insights and truths are involved in jettisoning the story of the Fall of creation.

Some may argue that I place too much weight on one particular story, but it hardly needs to be pointed out that the gospel writers (or more accurately compilers and redactors) wove together stories and fragments of narrative into what we now know as "canonical gospels." The genre of narrative lies at the heart of the Judeo-Christian tradition. The story of the Fall is inextricably related to the story of redemption; the one is impossible without the other. The question that should be before us is whether the ethical treatment of the nonhuman is possible at all without a narrative of messianic expectation. If we, and all creation, have nothing fundamentally to hope for—according to God's own promise—what can be the point of ethical striving?

It is therefore unsurprising that the frequent backcloth to this theological issue is the intensely practical question, namely, what, or whom, are we to eat? If "eat and get eaten" is the moral law of the universe, or if predation is "beautiful," there can be no moral imperative to live without injury. The truth is that human beings can now approximate the peaceable kingdom by living without killing sentients for food. Whether this has always been possible is something about which, at worst, I am doubtful; at best, I have an open mind. But whatever the past complexity, I believe that we should now rejoice at the fact that so many of our human contemporaries can live without killing sentients in order to eat—and eat well. Not only should we act generously in accordance with the moral freedom that we now enjoy but—most especially—we should learn the deep theological message implicit in its contemporary realization: We are the species who can dream divine-like dreams and by divine grace actualize them. Humans are the one species capable of continuing the story of God incarnate.

4

The Rights
of God's
Creatures

There is no disputing that in some quarters at least the whole notion of animal rights is unpopular, even the subject of derision.
It is difficult actually to think of any reforming movement that has
not had a bad press: The early "abolitionists" against the slave
trade certainly did; so also, more recently, have suffragettes, fem-
inists, and civil rights advocates. It would be silly to suppose that
all animal advocates are saints or beyond criticism. I have been
outspoken in my own criticism of the movement from time to
time. But I also have to say that I have met many deeply caring,
conscientious, and sensitive people who work sacrificially and
unstintingly for the cause of animals. I don't mind admitting that
their care has personally sustained me during many dark hours.

It is vexing, therefore, to find animal advocates the general target of vilification, most usually by one or more spokespeople for
agencies that support, or have something to gain by, animal
abuse. That their criticisms are given prominence is of course not
accidental—the power of the vested interests they represent is
enormous. People need to beware of headlines and search out the
truth for themselves. In what follows I respond to one sort of attack, not just that animal advocates are "extremists" (the usual
kind of remark designed to put a stop to further thought) but
specifically the claim that animal rights have no theological basis.

Former U.S. Secretary of Health and Human Services Louis Sullivan told a Vatican conference that animal rights "extremists"
threaten the future of health research, and that churches "cannot
remain on the periphery in this struggle . . . Any assertion of moral

equivalence between humans and animals is an issue that organized religion must refute vigorously and unambiguously." Sullivan went on to say that world religious leaders possess the authority to "affirm the necessity of appropriate and human uses of animals in biomedical research."[1]

At first sight, Sullivan has backed a winner. What better than conservative theology and who better than conservative churches to respond to the rallying call for human superiority over animals—even and especially if this "superiority" involves inflicting pain and suffering? Christian theology has, it must be admitted, served long and well the oppressors of slaves, women, and animals. Only 138 years ago, William Henry Holcombe wrote confidently of slavery as the "Christianization of the dark races."[2] It took 1,900 years for theologians to question seriously the morality of slavery, and even longer the oppression of women. Keith Thomas reminds us that over the centuries theologians debated "half frivolously, half seriously, whether or not the female sex had souls, a discussion which closely paralleled the debate about animals." Apparently the Quaker George Fox encountered some who thought women had "no souls, no more than a goose."[3]

Who better to look to then but the Roman Catholic Church, which in its approved *Dictionary of Moral Theology* of 1962 confidently proclaims that "Zoophilists often lose sight of the end for which animals, irrational creatures, were created by God, viz., the service and use of man . . . In fact, Catholic moral doctrine teaches that animals have no rights on the part of man."[4] In practice, Catholic countries are among the worst in the world as far as animals are concerned. Bullfighting and the Spanish fiestas in which animals are gratuitously mutilated (with the compliance of priests and nuns) are examples of how historical theology lives on. Surely Sullivan could not have chosen a more agreeable ally in his fight against "extremists" who believe that animals have rights.

And yet, there are signs that Christian theology and Christian churches cannot be so easily counted upon to support the standard line that humans are morally free to do as they like with animals. Anglican Archbishop Donald Coggan in 1977 stated the unthinkable: "Animals, as part of God's creation, have rights which must be respected. It behoves us always to be sensitive to their needs and to the reality of their pain."[5] Archbishop Robert Runcie went further in 1988 and specifically contradicted historical anthropocentrism. His words deserve to be savored:

> The temptation is that we will usurp God's place as Creator and exercise a *tyrannical* dominion over creation . . . At the present time, when we are beginning to appreciate the wholeness and interrelatedness of all that is in the cosmos, preoccupation with humanity will seem distinctly parochial . . . too often our theology of creation, especially here in the so-called "developed" world, has been distorted by being too man-centered. We need to maintain the value, the preciousness of the human by affirming the preciousness of the nonhuman also—of all that is. For our concept of God forbids the idea of *a cheap creation*, of a throwaway universe in which everything is expendable save human existence . . . The value, the worth of natural things is not found in Man's view of himself but in the goodness of God who made all things good and precious in his sight . . . As Barbara Ward used to say, "We have only one earth." Is it not worth our love?[6]

Even at the very center of conservative theology there are indications of movement. The Pope's 1964 encyclical *Sollicitudo Rei Socialis* speaks of the need to respect "the nature of each being" within creation. It underlines the modern view that the "dominion granted to man . . . is not an absolute power, nor can one speak of a freedom to 'use and misuse,' or to dispose of things as one pleases."[7]

It would be silly to pretend that Pope John Paul II and Archbishops Coggan and Runcie are card-carrying members of the animal rights movement (there are no membership cards in any case). Yet for Sullivan, desperately hoping for moral assurance in the face of animal rights "extremists," these cannot be encouraging signs. Is the ecclesiastical bastion of human moral exclusivity really going to tumble? Might there be, in fifty or a hundred years, a Roman encyclical defending the worth, dignity, and rights of the nonhuman world? The *National Catholic Reporter* noted that Pope John Paul II had only "cautiously" defended animal experimentation. In 1982, the paper recalled, the Pope argued that "the diminution of experimentation on animals, which has progressively been made ever less necessary, corresponds to the plan and well-being of all creation."[8] The true reading of Sullivan's overture might be not confidence but desperation. Perhaps the most worrying thing for Sullivan is that the churches *won't* remain on the periphery in this struggle.

Sullivan has a counterpart in the United Kingdom: former agriculture minister and Roman Catholic John Selwyn Gummer, who tried to bolster the meat trade by asserting that vegetarianism is a "wholly unnatural" practice. Like Sullivan, he thought Christian theology would be of some help—in his case, against five million British vegetarians. "I consider meat to be an essential part of the diet," argued Gummer. "The Bible tells us that we are masters of the fowls of the air and the beasts of the field and we very properly eat them."[9]

Alas, biblical theology cannot be so easily wheeled in to rescue the minister of agriculture. The creation saga in Genesis 1 does indeed give humans dominion over animals (v. 28) but just one verse later commands vegetarianism (vv. 29–31). As Karl Barth observed, "Whether or not we find it practicable and desirable, the diet assigned to men and beasts by God the Creator is vegetarian."[10] Bystanders may marvel at how Gummer could in all innocence hurl himself not at the weakest but at the strongest part of his enemy's armor.

Sullivan and Gummer seem united in the view that if theology is to speak on animal rights, it will speak not on the side of the oppressed but on behalf of the oppressor. Indeed, the view somehow seems to have spread that there can be no mainstream theological basis for animal rights. As well as accusing the movement of being "philosophically flawed and obscurantistic—based on ignorance and emotion, not reason and knowledge—and ultimately antihuman and even anti-animal," the magazine *Eternity*, produced by Evangelical Ministries Inc., claimed that "The true religious underpinning of animal-rights activists is a kind of vague neopantheism."[11]

To begin to construct an adequate theological understanding of animals, we should recall Runcie's statement about the value, "the preciousness of the nonhuman." Secular thinkers are free to be agnostic about the value of the nonhuman creation. They could argue, for example, that creation has value only insofar as humankind is benefited or insofar as other creatures can be classed as utilities. Not so, however, for Christians. If, as Runcie observes, "our concept of God forbids the idea of a cheap creation" because "the whole universe is a work of love" and "nothing which is made in love is cheap," Christians are precluded from a purely humanistic, utilitarian view of animals. This point will sound elementary, but its implications are profound.

At its most basic it means that animals must not be viewed simply as commodities, resources, tools, utilities for human use. If we are to grapple with real theology, we must abandon purely humanocentric perspectives on animals. What the use of animals may be to us is a totally separate question from what their value is to almighty God. To argue that the value and significance of animals in the world can be circumscribed by their value and significance to human beings is simply untheological. I make the point strongly because there seems to be the misconception—even and especially prevalent among the doctrinal advocates of Christian faith—that theological ethics can be best expressed by a well-meaning, ethically enlightened humanism. Not so. To attempt a theological understanding must involve a fundamental break with humanism, secular and religious. God alone is the source of the value of all living things.

This argument is usually countered by saying that if this is so, it should follow that *all* creation has value, so we cannot rate animals of greater value than rocks or vegetables, let alone insects or viruses. Increasingly this argument seems to be made by "conservationists" and "green thinkers" who want to exclude animals from special moral consideration. They argue that the value of animals, and therefore what we owe them, is really on a par with the value of natural objects such as trees or rivers. One can immediately see how this view falls in neatly with the emerging green view of "holistic interdependence" and holistic appeals to respect "earth as a whole." God loves the whole creation holistically, so it is claimed.[12]

But is it true that God loves everything *equally*? Not so, I think. Christian tradition clearly makes a distinction between humans and animals, and also between animals and vegetables. Scholars eager to establish the preeminence of humans in Scripture have simply overlooked ways in which animals exist alongside humans within the covenant relationship. The Spirit is itself the "breath of life" (Gen. 1:30) of both humans and animals. The Torah delineates animals within its notion of moral community. After having surveyed the ways in which animals are specifically associated, if not identified, with humans themselves, Barth concludes, "'O Lord, thou preservest man and beast' (Ps. 36:6) is a thread running through the whole of the Bible; and it first emerges in a way which is unmistakable when the creation of man is classified in Genesis 1:24f with that of the land animals."[13]

The second way in which my argument may be countered is by proposing that while animals have some value, it is incontestably less than the special value of humans. But this objection only adds fuel to my thesis. I, for one, do not want to deny that humans are unique, superior, even, in a sense, of "special value" in creation. Some secular animal rightists, it is true, have argued in ways that appear to eclipse the uniqueness of humanity. But Christian animal rights advocates are not interested in dethroning humanity. On the contrary, the animal rights thesis requires the reenthroning of humanity.

The key question is, what kind of king is to be reenthroned? Gummer's utterances show only too well how "dominion" has come to mean little more than despotism. But the kingly rule of which we are, according to Genesis, the vice-regents or representatives, is not the brutalizing regime of a tyrant. Rather, God elects humanity to represent and actualize the loving, divine will for all creatures. Humanity is the one species chosen to look after the cosmic garden (Gen. 2:15). This involves having power over animals. Yet the issue is not whether we have power over animals but how we are to use it.

It is here that we reach the christological parting of the ways. Secularists may claim that power is itself the sufficient justification for our use of it. But Christians are not so free. No appeal to the power of God can be sufficient without reference to the revelation of that power exemplified in Jesus Christ. Much of what Jesus said or did about slaves, women, or animals remains historically opaque. But we know the contours even if many of the details are missing. The power of God in Jesus is expressed in *katabasis*, humility, self-sacrifice, powerlessness. The power of God is redefined in Jesus as practical costly service extending to those who are beyond the normal boundaries of human concern: the diseased, the poor, the oppressed, the outcast. If humans are to claim a lordship over creation, then it can only be a lordship of service. There can be no lordship without service.

According to the theological doctrine of animal rights, then, humans are to be the servant species—the species given power, opportunity, and privilege to give themselves, nay sacrifice themselves, for the weaker, suffering creatures. According to Sullivan, the churches must refute "any assertion of moral equivalence between humans and animals." But I, for one, have never claimed any strict moral equality between humans and animals. I have always been a bit worried by Peter Singer's view that animal liberation consists of accepting "equal consideration of interests" between humans and animals.[14] In my view, what we owe animals is more than equal consideration, equal treatment, or equal concern. The weak, the powerless, the disadvantaged, the oppressed should not have equal moral priority but greater moral priority. When we minister to the least of all we minister to Christ himself. To follow Jesus is to accept axiomatically that the weak have moral priority. Our special value as a species consists of being of special value for others.

The relevance of such theology to animal rights should be clear. Readers will have noticed that I have here used the term "animal rights" rather than "animal welfare" or "animal protection." Some Christians are still apt to regard "rights" terminology as a secular import into moral theology. They are mistaken. The notion of rights was first used in explicitly theological contexts. Moreover, animal rights are explicitly a problem of Christian moral theology for this reason: Catholic scholasticism has specifically and repeatedly repudiated animal rights. It is the tradition, not its so-called modern detractors, that insists on the relevance of the concept of rights. The problem is only now compounded because, unaware of history, Christians want to talk boldly of human rights yet quibble about the language when it comes to animals.

For me the theological basis of rights is compelling. God is the source of rights, and indeed the whole debate about animals is precisely about the rights of the Creator. For this reason in *Christianity and the Rights of Animals* I used the ugly but effective term "theos-rights."[15] Animal rights language conceptualizes what is objectively owed the Creator of animals. From a theological perspective, rights are not something awarded, granted, won, or lost but something *recognized*. To recognize animal rights is to recognize the intrinsic value of God-given life.

I do not deny that the rights view involves a fundamental reorientation. This is one of its merits. The value of living beings is not something to be determined by human beings alone. Part of the reason rights language is so controversial is that people sense from the very outset that recognizing animal rights must involve personal and social change. Whatever else animal rights means it cannot mean that we can go on consuming their flesh, destroying their habitats, and inflicting suffering. Quite disingenuously some church people say that they do not "know" what "animal rights" are. Meanwhile, by steadfastly refusing to change their lifestyles, they show a precise understanding of what those rights are.

Earlier I compared the oppression of slaves and women to that of animals. Some may regard that comparison as exaggerated, even offensive, but at the heart of each reform movement has been a simple yet fundamental change of perception. Slaves should not be thought of as property but as human beings with dignity and rights. Women should not be regarded as second-class humans but as humans with dignity and rights. At the heart of the animal rights movement is a change of moral perception, simple, yet profound: Animals are not our property or utilities but living beings with dignity and rights.

One homely example may suffice. The university where I used to work was situated amid acres of eighteenth-century parkland. Wildlife abounded. From my study window I observed families of wild rabbits. Looking up from my word processor from time to time, I gazed in wonder, awe, and astonishment at these beautiful creatures. I sometimes said half-jokingly, "It is worth coming to the university for the rabbits." Occasionally I invited visitors to observe them. Some paused in conversation and said something like, "Oh yes," as though I had pointed out the dust on my bookshelves or the color of my carpet. What they saw was not rabbits. Perhaps they saw machines on four legs, "pests" that should be controlled, perhaps just other "things." It is difficult to believe that such spiritual blindness and impoverishment is the best that the superior species can manage.

Sullivan makes free with calling animal rightists "extremists." The reality is, however, that moral theology would hardly advance at all without visionaries and extremists, people who see things differently from others and plead God's cause even in matters that others judge insignificant. I don't think there are many moderates in heaven.

5

Animals as a Case of Theological Neglect

Criticism of animal rights is frequently heard in the media, but it is seldom that an archbishop gets involved in the debate or actually leads the attack. One of these unusual moments was when the Archbishop of York, John Habgood, contributed an article to *The Times* critical of animal rights. In this chapter, I give the substance of my response and explain why I thought his views misconceived and muddle-headed.

Must the churches be morally backward about animals? At the height of the national debate about live exports, the Archbishop of York protested *against* animal rights. As hundreds took to the streets to demonstrate for animal rights (specifically the right not to be cruelly exported), the Archbishop was adamant that they had none and that the protesters were misguided: "Talk of 'rights' seems to imply an absoluteness that is unsustainable in theory and dangerous in practice, in that it inflates moral claims to the point of inducing some protesters to disregard the legitimate claims of their fellow human beings."[1]

Such a significant interjection at a sensitive moment in public debate deserves scrutiny. The arguments are threefold. First: "Rights entail corresponding responsibilities, and both words imply the existence of a moral community within which there is some degree of shared recognition of the balance between them." Again: "[animals] do not form part of the same moral community with us; indeed they do not form part of any moral community, since they do not and cannot exercise any moral responsibility."[2] Notice the contractualism espoused here: Only members of a moral community who can exercise duties can have rights.

Popular commentators have followed this lead. Paul Johnson is emphatic: "There is no possibility of animals possessing rights unless they are conscious of duties."[3] Hugh Montefiore no less so: "Animals can no more have rights than they can discharge duties."[4]

For pragmatic and political purposes, such an argument may keep animal rights at bay, but at what cost? Contractualism which bases rights on the discharge of duties certainly excludes animals, but not only animals—also infants, the mentally disabled, comatose patients, a whole class of vulnerable, even innocent, human subjects. Is contractualism a self-evident platform for Christian ethics? If animals are to be pushed out of the "moral community" because they do not possess duties, logic demands that we do not stop there. No wonder historically the movement for the rights of animals has been so intertwined with the movement for the rights of children; contrary to prejudice, members of the Royal Society for the Prevention of Cruelty to Animals (RSPCA) helped found and support the National Society for the Prevention of Cruelty to Children (NSPCC).[5]

The second argument runs as follows: "As presumed 'rights' have multiplied, the mutuality between rights and responsibilities has diminished, and 'rights' are proclaimed for which nobody is, or could be, responsible . . . One consequence of this gradual devaluation of the concept is to make it less effective in those extreme circumstances where it is really needed. The right not to be tortured, for instance, should be regarded as absolute . . ." In short, claiming animal rights weakens human rights. But does it? Let us consider torture. I agree that such a right is indeed a very strong, if not an absolute, one. But how can such a right be advanced against the torturing of innocent human subjects that does not equally apply to animal subjects which are also, necessarily, morally innocent? Of course there are differences between human and animal subjects, sometimes important ones, but are there *morally relevant* ones? Consistency requires opposition to the torturing of any innocent subject, whether with duties (adults) or without (infants, mentally disabled, *and* animals).

The third argument goes as follows: "Nor is it clear, how, say, the rights of life and to be spared unnecessary suffering can have any meaning for wild animals outside a human context, except in terms of some general obligation on human beings to preserve the natural environment." If "human context" means the absence of "human moral agency," then this view is correct since nature is an amoral system. Amoral beings by definition cannot have duties to one another. If, however—and this seems more likely—it means that humans have no direct moral responsibility to wild animals because they are wild, it is surely mistaken. Do we then have no direct moral obligation to those wild animals we hunt for sport, or trap for their fur, or make captive for entertainment or research?

Habgood concludes, "To talk instead about our responsibility towards sentient creatures places the moral imperative where it belongs, namely in ourselves, and also allows scope for negotiating some reasonable balance of responsibilities between one group and another." Notice here the wholly humanocentric frame of moral reference. The assumption throughout is that humans alone are the source of moral obligation to animals. Astonishingly, there is not one line of reference to what we owe God the Creator—indeed no reference to God at all. What is utterly lost is any sense that animals are God's creatures, that we have an obligation to the Creator to respect what is created.

This omission would be readily forgivable if the author were simply another secular moralist for whom all moral obligations are, to a greater or lesser extent, humanistic negotiations. But for a Christian leader to advance a moral understanding of creatures without reference to their Creator is lamentable. Perhaps this is the reason churches seem unable to give any kind of lead about animals; they have no real theology to offer. To attempt a theological understanding of animals requires a radical break with humanism, both religious and secular. Humans are not the measure of the worth of all other creatures. The utility and value of other creatures to us is a totally separate question from what their value is to almighty God. A truly theocentric understanding of animals does not begin by assuming that the value of animals can be determined by moral negotiation, however desirable that may generally be, or that the worth of other creatures is deducible from human wants and needs.

As already noted, theories of animal rights are not without a theological basis: If God is the sovereign Creator, all rights in an absolute sense are God's. Rights language helps focus our attention on the value of what is given by the Creator in the sentient lives of other creatures. If it comes to "contractualism," there is only one contract: the divine covenant made not just with human beings but with all living beings.

Of course, rights discourse is difficult, even problematic. But so then is *all* moral discourse: Those who appeal too eagerly to "duties" frequently have no notion of how problematic any rational explication of duties is. The utilitarian and contractualist alternatives to rights theory bristle with difficulties, and until comparatively recently most Christian ethicists would have blushed at the idea that they could be so easily incorporated into mainstream theological ethics. I myself have been a stern critic of some of the more absolute claims made for rights theory, especially when it is suggested that rights is the *only* possible moral discourse or a wholly comprehensive one.[6]

But those who have pioneered the extension of rights language to animals deserve to have their arguments heard and met fairly. It is implausible to suggest, for example, that such theories weaken respect for human rights since the very criteria proposed ("subject of a life" or sentiency) so obviously include human subjects as well. More important, those who complain about animal rights fail to grasp the historical significance of such language. As already noted, the notion of animal rights has largely become the issue it is because Western thinking, influenced by the Christian tradition, has *denied* rights to animals while affirming them in the case of human beings. Whatever else the denial of rights has meant we should be clear that *in practice* it has meant that we have no objective moral obligation to them. Early anti-cruelty legislation in Britain was opposed precisely on the familiar Thomist grounds that animals had no rights.

The reason talk of rights is so readily dismissed, however, has little to do with comparative theory. It has to do with the underlying acceptance that there are strong, rather than weak, obligations to animals which may be expressed in terms of fundamental moral limits. The underlying ethical shift is away from the idea that animals can be classed as resources, commodities, means to human ends, here for our use, to the realization that as sentient beings, made by God, they have intrinsic value and worth. Rights language is especially appropriate in defense of the weak, the innocent, the vulnerable, and the unprotected—whether they be humans or animals. It is nothing short of tragic to see Christian leaders setting themselves against a contemporary moral sensitivity which can claim a solid theological, nay christological, basis. There is, as Newman saw, something Christ-like about the innocent suffering of animals.

Habgood assures us that he fully shares the concern of those who have coined the notion of animal rights, namely that "animals should be treated with respect and spared unnecessary cruelty." But the upshot of his argument belies this. Whenever any human interest conflicts with animals, their interests must, as a matter of course, be subordinated. Under the guise of rejecting animal rights, what is rejected is any serious competing claim to human moral supremacy. One of the reasons people speak of animal rights is precisely because they mean to challenge the right of humans to their massively cruel use of animals in virtually every quarter of life, whether it be for food, science, or sport.

Habgood writes of the need to negotiate "some reasonable balance of responsibilities" between humans and animals, but why then is it that archbishops appear unable *inter alia* to oppose hunting for sport, fur trapping for adornment, or even, most moderate of all, to support the demand that animals be transported no more than eight hours without rest, food, and water? Such unresponsiveness invites the conclusion that animal rightists are animal welfarists who mean it.

6

Animal Rights as Religious Vision

For me Jesus is the way, the truth, and the life. What is given in Jesus is, in my view, determinative of our understanding of the nature of God. I share John Austin Baker's conviction that the crucified Jesus is the most accurate picture of God the world has ever seen.[1] This does not mean, however, that there is no truth in any other religion or that other religious traditions are incapable of mediating a proper sense of God or of spiritual truth. When it comes to the ethical treatment of animals, we need to recognize frankly that some other religions have traditions of compassion that equal, even surpass, that of Christianity. In this chapter, I try to sketch some of the ways in which insights from a variety of religious traditions can be seen as implicitly or explicitly supportive of a new ethical sensitivity to animals.

During the last twenty-five years, we have witnessed the growth of a new socially reforming movement called the animal rights movement. Like others, this movement has been distinctly ideas-led. During the last twenty years there has been, as Andrew Rowan has pointed out, more philosophical discussion of the moral status of animals than there was during the previous two thousand years.[2] A revolution in ideas has been the major precursor to a fundamental shift of ethical sensibility.

I am reminded of a conversation between William Temple and his father, Frederick Temple, when William was a precocious schoolboy. At dinner one evening, William asked his father, "Why do not philosophers rule the world, Father? Would it not be a good thing if they did?" "They do," came the emphatic reply, "five hundred years after they are dead."[3] Almost without knowing it, we have inherited in Western culture certain ideas about animals which we seldom question and rarely scrutinize rationally. These ideas are almost entirely negative: Animals have no souls, they are not rational like humans, they are "put here" for our use. Each of these ideas has a long, predominantly Christian, history. Although many individual philosophers and thinkers have questioned these ideas, until quite recently they have gone unchallenged—at least politically and socially.

We are witnessing for the first time in Western history effective intellectual challenges to traditional views of animals based on these negative ideas. Although the media frequently present the animal rights movement as sentimental, antihuman, or anti-intellectual, the truth is almost entirely the reverse. The animal rights movement had its origin (in modern times) in the growth of the humanitarian movement in the nineteenth century which was, of course, concerned with improving living conditions for various oppressed subjects, children as well as animals—and has been spurred on during the last half-century at least by sustained philosophical and moral argument. Indeed, as early as 1977, the anti-animal rights philosopher Raymond Frey complained about the prevailing philosophical "orthodoxy" in favor of animal rights and vegetarianism.[4]

At the heart of the animal rights movement are, I suggest, two basic insights. The first we have already enumerated: It is that animals are not just commodities, resources, machines, things, means-to-human-ends, or beings here-for-our-use but rather sentient beings (capable of pain and suffering) with intrinsic value. The second insight is that there must be moral limits to what we may do to animals. This latter insight is most commonly expressed by saying that animals have "interests" or "rights." By positing animal rights, we insist that there are limits to what may be done to them morally. That doesn't mean, of course, that all animal rights are absolute (any more than it means that human rights are absolute), but it does mean that in normal situations at least there are certain limits that we should observe in our treatment of them. Clearly animal rights language is the language of strong moral obligation; it denotes checks and markers en route to a less exploitative way of living with nonhuman animals. Although our obligations to humans and animals are not identical, they are in essence the same *sort* of obligation.

These two insights—the apprehension of the intrinsic value of other sentient beings, and a keen sense of human moral limits in relation to them—have not been universally welcomed among religious people. Indeed, among Christians in particular there seems to be the most concerted opposition. To give just one example, in the journal *Trumpet Call*, published by the Peniel Pentecostal Church, the lead article argued that, "Meat eating and the acceptance that beasts are meant to serve humankind is not only justifiable in every moral consideration, but it is also biblical. The doctrinaire and unnatural decision to become vegetarian, or to put the rights of animals above those of man, is sinful and cannot be reconciled to a Christian life."[5] The assumption is that animal rights is essentially a secular philosophy compromising religious, specifically Christian, perspectives. And generally there seems no getting away from it; animal rights philosophy *does* pose some apparently sharp challenges to elements within not only Christian but also other religious worldviews as well.

Let me select just two. The first is *humanocentricity*. By this I mean humanocentricity (of a bad sort) in which duties are seen as things that apply primarily, if not exclusively, to human subjects. With the possible exception of the Jain tradition, and mindful that it is hazardous to generalize about the world's religious traditions, it nevertheless seems generally true that even within such traditions in which concern for animals is engaged it is principally done on the basis that such concern is secondary and peripheral to that central concern appropriate for human subjects. At the very least, although there are some shafts of light—principally though not exclusively from Eastern traditions—animal rights philosophy appears to have no obvious religious tradition to which it can appeal and in which it feels unambiguously at home.

The second is *hierarchy*. By this I mean the tendency within all religious traditions to grade forms of life in such a way that human life and well-being are always seen as intrinsically more significant and more important than those of any other species. According to the Aristotelian hierarchy virtually taken over by

St. Thomas Aquinas, within the Christian tradition there is something like an intellectual pyramid in creation, with humans placed at the top and the other animals in descending intellectual order. However difficult it may be to gauge the relative moral merits of other species, it must be clear that such hierarchical ordering by itself invariably leads to the disparagement of other (nonhuman) beings. We judge other beings by ourselves: our needs, definitions, aspirations, and complexes. Notwithstanding the need to make definitions and discriminations of various kinds, religious traditions have nearly always assumed and justified the moral priority of the human species.

Given these challenges, only two of which I have enumerated, it is perhaps not surprising that many religious people feel that animal rights represents a departure from at least some historically evolved religious perspectives. Or, ironically, some believe the very reverse, that animal rights is inseparable from a reprobate religious tendency—so-called "animal worship." And, it must be said, there have been some Christian critics of animal rights who have not shrunk from arguing just that.[6]

And yet it seems to me to be entirely superficial to maintain an absolute juxtaposition between animal rights insights and world religious traditions. Although on the whole such traditions have been heavily humanocentric and hierarchical in their thinking and practice (as invariably have been the societies in which they emerged and developed), it is also true that many of these same traditions contain what I can only call elements of an inclusive moral vision—inclusive, that is, of specifically nonhuman beings. Let me try to articulate three basic notions that seem especially relevant here.

In the first place, within theistic traditions—and here I think primarily of Judaism, Christianity, and Islam—there is the familiar idea that animals are with us *common creatures* of the same God. All beings, according to a theistic perspective, originate with a Creator who is loving, just, and holy. In theory this means that animals are not completely separate from us; there is a common ontological basis for all life. This view alone can provide a strong theoretical framework for the commonly articulated sense of kinship and affinity which many humans feel instinctively with the natural world and animals in particular. In the Qur'an, there is an explicit acknowledgment that animals form communities like us and that they, too, praise their Creator. "There is not an animal on earth, nor a bird that flies on its wings, but they are communities like you . . ." (6:38). In the Hebrew Bible, the covenant is made specifically not only with human beings but with Noah, his descendants, and all living creatures (Gen. 9:8). One of the sayings of the Prophet explicitly accepts that this covenant has implications for the way in which one species should treat another. He says, "When a snake appears in a dwelling place say to it: 'We ask you by the covenant of Noah and by the covenant of Solomon, son of David, not to harm us.' "[7] In the Christian tradition, the notion of St. Francis of Assisi that animals are our "brothers and sisters" in creation predates Darwin and the discoveries of evolution.

If a theistic perspective is engaged, it follows that human needs or estimations of the value of other creatures cannot be the main or sole criterion by which we can base our understanding of their moral worth. That animals are creatures of God must imply that they (nonhuman animals) have a moral worth in themselves. Although this is an elementary and hardly controversial implication of creation doctrine, its moral ramifications are rarely considered.

In the second place, in Indian traditions, principally Hinduism, Buddhism, and Jainism, there is the central idea of *ahimsa*—translated by Gandhi as "nonviolence" or "non-injury."[8] Although this idea is variously understood, its extension to nonhuman life forms has never been in doubt. This has given rise, as we all know, to traditions of vegetarianism and abstinence from animal protein. It is striking from a Western Christian perspective how traditions which often derive little from a belief in the Creator should so clearly have grasped what most Western theists have overlooked: the self-evident worth of all life itself. In Buddhism the principle of no killing, or harmlessness, constitutes the first precept. In the Hindu tradition, it has been claimed that "almost all the Hindu scriptures place strong emphasis on the notion that God's grace can be received by not killing his creatures or harming his creation . . ."[9] Indian religions have frequently laid before us the goal of living nonviolently with our nonhuman neighbors, and in that sense have invariably included animals directly within the moral circle, in a way in which Western religious traditions have not.

And yet the principle of respect for all life has not been entirely lost even in theistic traditions which are usually ambivalent about respect for animal life *per se*. One foundational text in this regard is Genesis 1:29, which requires vegetarianism. Although not formally requiring a meatless diet, Judaism has often viewed vegetarianism as the "ideal" diet commanded by God before humanity's descent into sin symbolized by the Fall and the flood. Although nonviolence toward animals has rarely been perceived as a Christian duty as such, the principle of *ahimsa* does find an echo in Albert Schweitzer's doctrine of reverence for life. The German word *Ehrfurcht*, correctly translated as "reverence" rather than simply "respect," preserves the religious, even mystical, aspect of Schweitzer's thought.

`   In the third place, almost all religious traditions have placed various emphases on the notion of *empathy* or *compassion* for those who suffer. "Kindness to any living creature will be rewarded" according to Muhammad.[10] The Jewish tradition forbids cruelty to animals, a view summarized in the Hebrew phrase *tsa'ar ba'alei chayim*, the biblically based injunction not to cause "pain to any living creature."[11] In accordance with this principle, Jews have consistently refused to participate in bloodsports, especially sport hunting. "Let a man feel hatred for no contingent being, let him be friendly, compassionate" declares the Lord Krishna in the *Bhagavad Gita*.[12] In Mahayana Buddhism, the Bodhisattva resolves to save all living things from the cycle of misery and death. This resolution is surely one of the most noble found within any religious tradition:

> I have made a vow to save all living beings . . . The whole world of living beings I must rescue, from the terrors of birth, of old age, of sickness, of death and rebirth . . . I must ferry them across the stream of Samsara. I myself must grapple with the whole mass of sufferings of all beings. To the limit of my endurance I will experience all the states of woe, found in any world system, all the abodes

of suffering. And I must not cheat all beings out of my store of merit. I am resolved to abide in each single state of woe for numberless aeons; and so I will help all beings to freedom . . . [13]

I know of no religious tradition that teaches indifference to suffering as a matter of principle. Indeed, the meritorious acts within almost all religious traditions consist in their relief of unnecessary suffering. Even within Christianity—in some ways the most humanocentric of all religions—dogmatic orthodoxy has had to coexist with the tradition of saints East and West who have befriended animals, showed compassion for them, and even engaged in heroic acts of protecting them from cruelty.

Now, it is important that these general remarks should not be misunderstood. I am not claiming that, rightly understood, all religious traditions are unambiguously favorable to animals, still less to a modern doctrine of animal rights. I am not claiming that all religions are on the side even of moderate animal welfare. But I am claiming that there are within almost all religious traditions notions concerning the status of animals—and of the nature of our moral obligation—that can aid a more imaginative appreciation of their individual worth and lend support to the notion of moral limits.

While I am the first to admit that a great deal of Christian history and theology has been neglectful and callous toward animals, it remains true that even here there are rich resources within Christianity for a deeper respect for animals as creatures of God. But as I have pursued my own work, I have become increasingly aware of other scholars and thinkers within other traditions working simultaneously for similar goals. Within Islam, the late Al-Hafiz B. A. Masri, former Imam of the Woking Mosque, spent his life working publicly for the welfare of animals. Masri was deeply convinced that Muslim doctrine required a compassionate view of animals. His book *Islamic Concern for Animals*, published in English and Arabic, has become a standard text. [14] Within Judaism, Richard Schwartz and Roberta Kalechofsky have been pioneers. Schwartz's book *Judaism and Vegetarianism* makes the case for vegetarianism derived from biblical teaching and the traditional mandate not to cause pain to animals.[15] Kalechofsky has edited a seminal collection titled *Judaism and Animal Rights,* which includes her own essay on how experiments on animals anticipated and paralleled experiments on human subjects.[16] Within Buddhism, Philip Kapleau, director of the Zen Center in New York, has been a leading advocate of Buddhist vegetarianism. His book *To Cherish All Life: A Buddhist Case for Becoming Vegetarian* takes issue with the Theravada tradition which sanctions meat eating, and argues that the Buddha was not only a vegetarian but admonished his followers to be so as well.[17]

Although it is wrong to suggest that religions are always the allies of animals, it is worth appreciating the religious, even mystical, insights in which the modern animal rights movement is grounded. The first of these is the mystical appreciation that what is given in the lives of other beings has intrinsic value—to be precise, a nonnegotiable, noninstrumentalist, nonutilitarian value. Such an insight, I suggest, finds its most natural home within a worldview in which humans are not the measure of all things or indeed the master of them. Similarly, the notion that there are moral limits to what we may do to animals presupposes a moral order in which human needs and wants are not by themselves the sole criterion of what is morally good. In other words, both animal rights insights belong morally to a *more than humanistic* view of the world. It is the worship of humanity, the deification of the human species itself, that prevents a proper understanding of animals, and indeed of ourselves. It is worth bearing in mind that if Western religion has been detrimental to animal rights, even more so has been the recent history of Western technology, which more than any other philosophy has regarded animals as machines and commodities.

It therefore seems to me to be possible to claim animal rights insights as at least a development of some notions which are implicit, if not explicit, in a religious way of looking at the world. Moral insight after all does not come from nowhere; all insight logically is rooted in a way of looking at the world. Some Christians seem astonishingly blinkered in their appreciation of their own tradition in this regard. After all, animal rightists have not invented the vision of the wolf lying down with the lamb in Isaiah 11:6, or the universal command to be vegetarian in Genesis 1:29, or indeed the vision of the earth in a state of childbirth awaiting its deliverance from suffering in Romans 8: in these, and in other ways, animal rightists can claim to be rediscovering and reactualizing visionary elements already present within the Western religious tradition.

What is urgently required is for religious people to reexamine and rediscover the riches from within their own respective traditions which enable a morally positive view of animals. The truth is that, until now, few within any of these traditions have seen the necessity or urgency of doing so. But if the animal rights movement is not to degenerate into just another fashionable secular movement divorced from the great traditions of religious thought, it is imperative that these great traditions engage with such insights in a thoughtful and reflective way. Arguably, within the Christian tradition at least, animal rights insights are correctives to a tradition which has failed to reflect sufficiently creatively on some of its own most cherished ideas. It is of course easy to deride the animal rights movement as "secular," but it has always seemed to me a great mistake to suppose that only religious people understand fully—or indeed fully reflect on—the basic insights of their own traditions.

My conclusion is that the basic insights of animal rights are consistent with many religious ideas and intuitions, and need to be brought into a much closer relationship with them. A spirituality that cannot or does not engage with contemporary moral movements is likely to discover itself increasingly irrelevant to people's deeply felt concerns. At the same time, moralism is not enough either. We need a spirituality that is open to new moral insights but which also saves us from the dangers of intolerance and self-righteousness. Moralism is not enough because for its very coherence and survival it depends upon a religious vision of how the world should be. The American naturalist Henry Beston in his book, *The Outermost House*, published in 1928, posed the challenge in this way: "We need another and wiser and perhaps a more mystical concept of animals . . . They are not our brethren, they are not underlings; they are other nations, caught with ourselves in the net of life and time, fellow prisoners of the splendor and travail of the earth."[18]

7

Why Church Teaching Perpetuates Cruelty

Few Christians like to see the teaching of the Church criticized. At a time when there are so many mindless attacks on Christianity, it is hardly surprising if some react defensively, even intemperately, to criticism. I have received furious letters from Christians who are upset when I venture to criticize particular church traditions that are insensitive or callous toward animals. Some Christians argue that in an ecumenically sensitive age one should as a matter of principle refrain from all criticism of churches, especially those to which one doesn't personally belong. I have never taken that view. It has always seemed to me a false ecumenism to think that the cause of unity can be served by disguising or ignoring important issues.

More important, as I see it, all Christian churches have to be judged and weighed from time to time in the light of the Gospel. The churches seek to proclaim the Gospel, and not the reverse. It is a great mistake to deify our church traditions as though they represent the final word of God or are infallible. Criticism of the Church—in all its manifestations—seems to me to be a Christian duty if we are not to make the mistake of idolatry. In my time I have in turn been critical of almost all church traditions, whether they be Roman Catholic or Protestant, and I intend as a matter of obedience to the Gospel to go on doing so.

In this chapter, I give one example of how church teaching helps perpetuate animal abuse. It gives me no joy to do this, and I would much rather be able to give a wholly positive assessment of the record of all the churches. The reason I select the *Catholic*

Catechism for special scrutiny is because it represents in a clear and dramatic way how unenlightened official Christian teaching still is about animal welfare.

Many concerned for animals have expressed shock and disbelief at reports that have come their way concerning the new *Catholic Catechism* and its teaching on animals. Commissioned by Pope John Paul II and ten years in the making, the *Catechism* constitutes the *official* teaching of the Roman Catholic Church on faith and morals. I stress the word "official" here because while it is possible to find individual Catholic figures, even saints, bishops, and teachers, who have historically said or done things favorable to animals, they do not necessarily represent the "official" line. Indeed, they may be at variance with it. Many animal advocates, unaware of this, assume that this or that bishop, cardinal, or saint speaks unambiguously for the Catholic view. The truth is, only that which conforms to the teaching authority (*magisterium*) of the Catholic Church truly—and "officially"—represents authentic Catholic teaching—hence, the importance of the *Catechism*. It constitutes an authoritative update of the official Catholic position on a wide range of theological and ethical issues, including the official position on animals.

The section on animals is actually quite small: only four paragraphs. Located within overall discussion of the seventh commandment, it is titled "Respect for the Integrity of Creation" and reads as follows:

> The seventh commandment enjoins respect for the integrity of creation. Animals, like plants and inanimate beings, are by nature destined for the common good of past, present and future humanity. Use of the mineral, vegetable and animal resources of the universe cannot be divorced from respect for moral imperatives. Man's dominion over inanimate and other living beings granted by the Creator is not absolute; it is limited by concern for the quality of life of his neighbor, including generations to come; it requires a religious respect for the integrity of creation.
>
> *Animals* are God's creatures. He surrounds them with his providential care. By their mere existence they bless

him and give him glory. Thus men owe them kindness. We should recall the gentleness with which saints like St. Francis of Assisi or St. Philip Neri treated animals.

God entrusted animals to the stewardship of those whom he created in his own image. Hence it is legitimate to use animals for food and clothing. They may be domesticated to help man in his work and leisure. Medical and scientific experimentation on animals, if it remains within reasonable limits, is a morally acceptable practice since it contributes to caring for or saving human lives.

It is contrary to human dignity to cause animals to suffer or die needlessly. It is likewise unworthy to spend money on them that should as a priority go to the relief of human misery. One can love animals; one should not direct to them the affection due only to persons.[1]

The first paragraph reflects a new kind of ecological sensitivity already noted in the encyclical *Sollicitudo Rei Socialis* in which the Pope argued that the "dominion granted to man . . . is not an absolute power, nor can one speak of a freedom to 'use and misuse,' or to dispose of things as one pleases."[2] But note that here, all creation, including animals, is destined for ". . . humanity." There is no suggestion that it is wrong *in itself* to use sentient beings because they can be harmed or violated. Indeed, elsewhere in the *Catechism*, the ecological gloss is removed and the point made emphatically: "He [God] destined all material creatures for the good of the human race."[3] Thus, while this paragraph may appear sympathetic to eco-concerns, overall the *Catechism* still retains a strongly instrumentalist view of creation. The moral imperative is concerned with looking after creation *for humanity* and *for their* future generations.

The second paragraph contains the most positive theology of all about animals. They are God's creatures; they are cared for by God. "By their mere existence they bless him and give him glory." Hence, humans owe them "kindness" after the example of the saints.

Here the *Catechism* edges toward the view that because animals exist for God, they therefore have value independent of human wants and desires. Undoubtedly, this view constitutes an advance in Catholic thinking. Although placed generally within an instrumentalist context, it recognizes—implicitly at least—that animals have some intrinsic value. Most important of all, it seems that animals are for the first time included within the sphere of *direct* moral duty: We owe them something, namely "kindness." What an advance this is on the attitude of Pope Pius IX and previous Catholic textbooks that have straightforwardly denied that we have direct duties to animals.

But from this moral high point the following two paragraphs are downhill all the way. Paragraph three maintains that as humans are made in God's image and given stewardship, we may use animals for human purposes—quite specifically, for food and clothing, for domestication and labor, and for experimentation. "Medical and scientific experimentation on animals, if it remains within reasonable limits, is a morally acceptable practice since it contributes to caring for or saving human lives." Thus, despite the previously implied view that animals have an independent value because of their worth to God, the *Catechism* now goes on specifically to endorse our current use of animals in many key respects.

The final paragraph makes the position all too clear: The only criterion of moral use is human benefit and dignity. "It is contrary to human dignity to cause animals to suffer or die needlessly." Note that it is not wrong to cause animals to suffer and die because such activity harms the animals themselves and is therefore an offense to God. No; it is wrong solely because it is an affront to *human dignity*. Note also the caveat "needlessly." It is wrong to cause suffering only when it is "needless," that is, according to the logic of the Catechism, when it is divorced from human benefit, gain, or advantage. When looked at objectively, the range and force of this prescription is very limited. It may conceivably rule out some forms of cruel sports (note that the use of animals for entertainment is not specifically listed as one of the legitimate uses of animals), but if there is human benefit involved, or if it can be argued that such activities are not contrary to "human dignity," the presumption must be that they are morally acceptable. This one line alone lets in—that is, justifies—almost all we currently do to animals, save perhaps hideous cruelty perpetrated by the deranged.

The second line of this fourth paragraph is telling: "It is likewise unworthy to spend money on them [animals] that should as a priority go to the relief of human misery." Concern for animals (as represented by charitable giving) must be utterly secondary as a matter of principle to concern for human suffering. Notice also the way in which this line bolsters a familiar Catholic prejudice against animal welfare—namely, that it is wrong to be concerned about animals when humans are suffering in the world. The idea that we shouldn't spend money on animals that could go on human welfare may sound right until we think through the implications. In practice it would mean that we shouldn't spend *any* money on animal welfare until *all* human misery has been alleviated. What is worrying here is that the *Catechism opposes* animal welfare to human welfare. Concern for animals becomes officially second-class, marginal, peripheral. In short, this view plays off human welfare *against* animal welfare; it invites a moral juxtaposition in which animals always come off second best.

The final sentence is no less revealing: "One can love animals; one should not direct to them the affection due only to persons." At first sight it might appear bizarre to be given permission by the Catholic Church to love animals; but from the traditional Scholastic perspective, originating with St. Thomas Aquinas, one had no duty to love animals.[4] That we can love animals but not in the way we love humans is in one sense, of course, obviously true. We all know cases where human love of animals is sentimental or disproportionate. But the *Catechism* gives the unfortunate impression that even altruistic love of animals is misdirected or disproportionate.

It is a poor theology that wants to limit love in the world today. Any form of love can be cranky or obsessive. But why should the love of animals be singled out? There is a subtext to the *Catechism* which goes like this: Animals don't really matter in themselves. Don't waste precious human resources on them. Love them if you must, but not too much.[5] Effectively, while allowing the love of animals in principle, the *Catechism* reaffirms the traditional suspicion that affection for animals is disordered or disproportionate, especially if it in any way approximates the intensity of love between humans. Indeed, it arguably reaffirms the earlier Scholastic view that friendship is also only possible between humans, since animals are not, according to traditional Catholic thinking, "persons."

What then should be our final judgment on the *Catechism*? Looking positively (as hard as we can), we can say that at least animals are recognized as God's creatures and as having some worth independently of human beings. There is the new official acknowledgment that we owe animals kindness. Causing animals to suffer or die can conceivably—in some rarefied circumstances—be wrong.

Against this has to be set its sheer illogicality and permissiveness. It is illogical to acknowledge that animals have some independent worth to God and then practically subscribe to a wholly instrumentalist understanding of their status as resources for human use. When analyzed, it becomes clear that human utility or benefit alone can justify almost everything we now do to animals. Conspicuous by its absence is any reaffirmation of the view sometimes held within Catholic tradition that cruelty to animals is an intrinsic evil or an injustice to the animals themselves. In short, despite its limited overtures to animal welfare, the *Catechism* reaffirms a ruthless and dogmatic humanocentrism. In practice, it is not one step forward; it is two steps backward. This present Pope—as represented by the *Catechism*—will go down in history as the one who made concern for animals officially second-class.

Some nonreligious people reading this may say to themselves: So what? The Catholic Church has an unenlightened view of animals—but why should I be concerned about it?

I suggest it must be of concern to all animal advocates because the battle for animals will not, cannot, be won while major institutions in our society hold antiprogressive views on animals. The power of the Catholic Church is immense in the world today; this *Catechism* formally aligns that great religious institution with those who want to exploit animals—among other things—as laboratory tools. We should not deceive ourselves: The *Catechism* represents a major moral victory by the biotechnological establishment. It has received effective and official endorsement by the largest Christian organization in the world.

Let us also be clear what this means in practice in the world to-day for animals themselves. The result of putting animals in the theological second division is that they continue to receive second-class treatment. All churches have a terrible record on animals. In Spain, no Catholic authority opposes bullfighting; in Canada, Anglican and Roman Catholic bishops support fur trapping and seal hunting; in Norway, bishops and priests defend whaling; in Ireland, Catholic priests go hare coursing; in England, the General Synod will not oppose hunting on church land.

From my own perspective, as a Christian priest, this has to be a day for tears. There is so much good theology which could help liberate animals from human oppression; so much that could be done to foster a spirit of Christian compassion for animals within the churches; so many courageous and saintly voices in the tradition which have been set aside.

Just think how once, at the beginning of our movement in England, religious figures took the lead in spearheading public opposition to, for example, vivisection. In 1876 not only Lord Shaftesbury but also Cardinal Manning—two outstanding Christians of their day—founded the first antivivisection society in the world, the Victoria Street Society, together with Frances Power Cobbe and Dr. George Hoggan. Those early activists against vivisection included almost the entire ecclesiastical elite: the Archbishop of York, the Primate of Ireland, Lord Chief Justice Coleridge, and the Bishops of Winchester, Exeter, Salisbury, Manchester, Bath and Wells, Gloucester and Bristol, Hereford, St. Asaph, and Derry, among others.[6]

What then must be done? It is absolutely vital that all who care for animals make known their opposition to this *Catechism*. Catholics should make known their views in writing to their priest, bishop, archbishop, and to the Pope himself. It is also vital that letters are published in the religious press engendering church debate about animals. Also others need to write to the Catholic hierarchy to make known their disappointment and sadness at the failure of that church to take justice for animals seriously. Remember: Silence will be interpreted as consent. It is not inconceivable that the *Catechism* will be revised, at least over the next ten years. Local catechisms can be drawn up which, while based on the common *Catechism*, can stress the more positive aspects of traditional Catholic teaching.

For myself, I refuse to give up the struggle first begun by our great Christian forebears in the animal protection movement. I have dedicated my life to making some contribution to the day when animals will be given their rightful place in the official teaching of *all* the churches. As a precursor to emancipating the animals, some of us will have to emancipate the churches from their unchristian attitudes. I'm reminded of the line from Martin Buber: "Nothing is apt to mask the face of God so much as religion."[7]

8

The Christ-like Innocence of Animals

In the previous chapter I was unsparingly critical of current Catholic teaching about animals. All Christian traditions, however, contain resources for looking at animals in a positive way, and the Catholic tradition is certainly no exception.[1] Reference has already been made to the Christ-like innocence of animals. Here I show how one Catholic theologian pioneered this striking notion in a way that both goes to the heart of the redeeming work of Christ and also anticipates one central concern of modern-day animal advocates. In so doing, I chart an alternative route the Catholic tradition could have taken with regard to animals, as represented by one of its most celebrated theologians. In contrast to the "either/or" view of the *Catholic Catechism*, this approach helps us to appreciate the *common* vulnerability of both humans and animals.

"It is positively immoral to be concerned about animals when humans are suffering in the world." This comment recently offered to me represents the very worst of traditional moral theology. It provides a way in which ethical questions about animal suffering can be theologically brushed aside. Those who articulate this line—and I'm sorry to say it has found its way into many official textbooks of moral theology—frequently use it as a mental stop to thinking seriously about animals.

Its credibility depends of course upon an absolute theoretical separation of the suffering of animals and the suffering of humans. Human suffering is judged to be in a class of its own; animal suffering is something different. Can such a separation be justified theologically? I don't think so.

It was decisively answered in a little-known sermon preached by John Henry Newman when he was Vicar of St. Mary's University Church, Oxford, in 1842.[2] Newman's argument deserves reflection. Preaching on Good Friday on the suffering of the Lamb of God, Newman begins, "Since then Scripture compares [Christ] to this inoffensive and unprotected animal, we may without presumption or irreverence take this image [of the lamb] as a means of conveying to our minds those feelings which our Lord's suffering should excite within us. I mean consider how very horrible it is to read the accounts which sometimes meet us of cruelty inflicted upon brute animals." And he thunders, "For what was this but the very cruelty inflicted upon our Lord?"

What should "move our very hearts and sicken us," according to Newman, is the realization that animals are morally innocent, "that they have done no harm. Next that they have no power whatever of resisting; it is the cowardice and tyranny of which they are the victims which makes their suffering so especially touching . . . there is something so very dreadful, so satanic in tormenting those who have never harmed us and who cannot defend themselves, who are utterly in our power, who have weapons neither of offence nor defence that none but very hardened persons can endure the thought of it . . ."

And Newman concludes, "Think then, my brethren, of your feelings at cruelty practiced on brute animals, and you will gain one sort of feeling which the history of Christ's Cross and Passion ought to excite within you."[3] The eloquence and passion of Newman's denunciation of cruelty may surprise us.

We have come to accept as a matter of course the increasingly sophisticated and ruthless use of animals in our society. Hardly ever nowadays are serious Christian voices raised against our massive exploitation of animals. And yet while his message was as radical as any anti-cruelty sermon ever preached, Newman was actually only repeating, albeit in a heightened form, the traditional Christian opposition to cruelty.

What Newman, of his genius, provides is the decisive theological reasoning as to *why* cruelty is unchristian. Note the

christological thrust: Christ is the innocent victim *par excellence.*
The Cross of Christ is nothing less than God's identification with
innocent suffering. Sensitivity to undefended suffering, unprotected suffering, undeserved and unmerited suffering should
arise directly out of reflection upon the awfulness of crucifixion.

With the question "What was this but the very cruelty inflicted
upon our Lord?" Newman posits the moral equivalence of the infliction of suffering upon Christ with the infliction of suffering
upon innocent animals. It follows that to be for Christ is to be
against the "satanic" (Newman's own word) oppression of innocents. Never has any theologian offered such a penetrating exegesis of the scriptural notion of "the Lamb of God."

The moral upshot of Newman's line is that cruelty inflicted
upon animals is intrinsically evil—as intrinsically evil as cruelty
inflicted upon vulnerable humans such as children. The key point
is the notion of moral innocence. Like children—except arguably
even more so—animals, in the words of C. S. Lewis, "cannot deserve pain or be improved by it."⁴ To inflict suffering on an innocent being save arguably for that one individual's own good (for
example, in a medical operation) incurs moral evil.

One of the reasons so many Christians will have difficulty with
Newman's thesis is that they will immediately perceive that vast
changes would need to take place in human society if this norm
were seriously adhered to. The truth is that we make animals suffer for food, for clothes, for sport, and for science. There is hardly
an area of human life in which we do not systematically oppress
the innocents of whom Newman spoke. Indeed, we may guess
that the reports of suffering to which he himself refers in his sermon were probably references to the anti-vivisection debate in
Oxford which raged throughout most of the 1800s.⁵

But consequentialism is not enough. It is not sufficient theologically to justify our cruelty to animals simply on the grounds
that such suffering is useful to us. One of the valuable aspects of
the papal encyclical, *Veritatis Splendor,* was not only its reaffirmation of the category of "intrinsically evil acts" but also its utter rejection of consequentialism as an adequate basis for theological
ethics. "If acts are intrinsically evil, a good intention or particular
circumstances can diminish their evil, but they cannot remove it.

They remain 'irremediably' evil acts; *per se* and in themselves they are not capable of being ordered to God and to the good of the person."[6]

I suggest that such must be concluded of all acts that involve the deliberate infliction of pain and suffering upon animals (except where such actions are for the individual's own benefit), no matter the consequences and no matter how honorable the intentions of those who inflict it.

In the past, Catholic theology has often been content with simply pointing out how cruelty can brutalize human beings, and how because of these likely effects cruelty should be discouraged. There is certainly something to be said for this view. There is now an increasing amount of evidence in the United States of the direct link between cruelty to children and cruelty to animals.[7] Recently the Washington Humane Society put out a poster featuring the split faces of a child and a dog with this caption running across: "The Dad who comes home and kicks the dog is probably just warming up."[8]

But we must beware of falling into yet another consequentialist trap and arguing that evil can be opposed only on grounds other than that it is evil. Newman's mystical identification of Christ's suffering with the innocent suffering of animals may appear a flimsy basis on which to wage a worldwide Catholic crusade against animal cruelty; but we need to remind ourselves of Newman's even more insistent view concerning the development of doctrine.[9]

A truly catholic conscience is one that is always open to the multilayered truth represented by the outstretched hands on the Cross. The Newman doctrine of the Christ-like innocence of animals awaits its full reception in the Catholic Church.

PART 2

Disengaging from the Works of Darkness

9

Overview:
The Dream
Dreams Us

At the heart of the Christian Gospel is the dream of universal peace, a world where humans are no longer violent and cruel to other creatures. Imagining such a world is such a difficult and demanding thing that it is not surprising that many, even Christians, deride the very possibility. But in my view this dream—precisely because it is God's dream—has great power to energize moral endeavor. The urgent question is: How can sinful human beings begin to realize this dream?

In my view, animal advocates need two things: vision and pragmatism—not one at the expense of the other but both together. In this chapter I defend a program of progressive disengagement, both social and personal, from animal exploitation as the Christian strategy to realize the biblical dream of peace. Human striving cannot, of course, by itself achieve the dream, but we can cooperate with God's Spirit in the realization of the divine dream. It is not just that we dream and strive to achieve our dreams; it is rather that the dream dreams us.

Imagine a scene. It's a hot, sunny, sweltering day. The date is 1963; August 28 to be precise. The place is the Lincoln Memorial in Washington D.C. The time is late in the afternoon. You are one of 250,000 people who have come from all over America. You hear these words:

> I have a dream that one day men will rise up and come to
> see that they are made to live together as brothers.

The speaker is, of course, Martin Luther King. He goes on to make an impassioned plea for civil rights.

> I still have a dream this morning that one day every Negro in this country will be judged on the basis of his character rather than the color of his skin, and that every man will respect the dignity and worth of human personality. I still have a dream today that one day the idle industries of Appalachia will be revitalized, and that the empty stomachs of Mississippi will be filled, and that brotherhood will be more than a few words at the end of a prayer but rather the first order of business on every legislative agenda.

And he concludes:

> I still have a dream today that war will come to an end, that men will beat their swords into ploughshares and their spears into pruning hooks, that nation will no longer rise up against nation, neither will they study war any more. I still have a dream today that one day the lamb and the lion will lie down together and every man will sit under his own vine or fig tree and none shall be afraid.[1]

Martin's words have long passed into history. We are all aware, of course, how it was that Martin's speech encapsulated the hope of a generation; how it was the flash point of a movement, of a long, hard, and continuing movement for social justice. It reflected a conflict which has been faced and fought—at least with some success, despite many failures—all over the world. Much has yet to be done, but how Martin would have been heartened by much of what we take for granted today.

Martin was, of course, a dreamer. I do not mean by that someone who indulges fancy or who fantasizes about the future. Rather, I mean someone who sees—as a visionary—new worlds. Every social reform movement has had its dreams and its dreamers. We, too, in the animal movement have not lacked either.

Imagine another scene. The date is June 16, 1824. The place is the Old Slaughterer's Coffee House in St. Martin's Lane in old

London. A meeting is taking place called by a largely unknown Anglican cleric, Arthur Broome. Those in attendance (at this or subsequent meetings) include two members of the House of Lords, six members of the House of Commons, including Richard Martin and William Wilberforce, and four Anglican clergy.[2] The purpose of the meeting is to found the first national animal welfare society in the world.[3] Two weeks later, the first "Prospectus" of the Society for the Prevention of Cruelty to Animals was published. Written by Arthur Broome himself, it begins as follows:

> In an age so enlightened as the present it is less extraordinary that a Society should be formed for the Prevention of Cruelty to Animals, than that such a Society should be of comparatively recent establishment. Our country is distinguished by the number and variety of its benevolent institutions—a tender care for our suffering brethren of every colour and complexion, of every clime and country, of every age and condition of life, has been nurtured by many admirable institutions, all actuated by one common philanthropy, and all breathing the pure spirit of Christian charity and good-will towards mankind.

The second paragraph runs as follows:

> But shall we stop here? Is the moral circle perfect so long as any power of doing good remains? Or can the infliction of cruelty on any being which the Almighty has endowed with feelings of pain and pleasure, consist with genuine and true benevolence? Morality consists in the desire, rationally directed, to promote general happiness, and secondly to diminish general pain, and it cannot be contended that the operation of a principle, so glorious to man, should not be made to embrace in its effects, the whole of animal life.[4]

A number of things may strike us about this early statement of the philosophy of animal protection. We may wince a little at its self-confident, even triumphalist nationalism. We may find its

73

assumingly self-evident principle of morality a little strained. We may detect more than a hint of self-congratulation behind the words "[I]n an age so enlightened as the present," or as in a little later on, "[it] might thus have been expected that a nation so great and generous, *as our own confessedly is*."[5] But one thing we cannot fail to miss: the visionary, dream-like perspective here espoused. Despite the document's astonishing claim to "disclaim all visionary and overstrained views in the pursuit of [its] purpose" (all the more amazing when one considers that two years earlier saw—after vigorous opposition—the first and only anti-cruelty legislation in the world, but that confined solely to cattle),[6] the first prospectus of the then SPCA exudes a certitude of moral righteousness in the humane cause and—no less significant—in its eventual triumph. The object of the Society was nothing less than "the mitigation of animal suffering, and the promotion and expansion of humanity towards . . . animated beings."[7]

Animal protectionists are the descendants of this dream. I have already drawn attention to the serious shortcomings of the Christian tradition when it comes to animals. And yet this tradition, which has provided the best (or at least the most successful) arguments against animals, is also the same tradition which gave birth to the humane movement in the nineteenth century. In perhaps the one and only line of understatement in the entire prospectus, it is pointed out that "much remains to be done towards the *entire accomplishment* of the humane views of those who in various ways have recommended the great moral and Christian obligation of kindness and compassion towards the brute creation," and it continues, "and *for this purpose* the present Society has been established."[8] Indeed, a little later the SPCA was to record in its minute book the declaration that "the proceedings of this Society are entirely based on the Christian Faith, and on Christian Principles."[9]

We are the descendants not only of a dream but also of a dreamer. It was a Christian minister, Arthur Broome, who founded the RSPCA. He became its first Secretary. He gave up his London church to work full-time unpaid for the Society. He was the first person to instigate the system of anti-cruelty inspectors—paid for out of his own pocket. He was the person who went to prison to pay for the Society's debts.[10] We do well to recognize the value of dreams and the courage of dreamers.

There is a great deal to be said, both morally and politically, for the art of dreaming. Looking back over 150 years of what we hope has been social progress, how obvious it now seems that the dreamers of emancipation, either for slaves, blacks, women, or children, had right on their side. So often history vindicates the dreamer, even if he or she is an object of scorn among contemporaries. Given the enormous changes in modern society, the dreamer of today can become the realist of tomorrow. Being "with it" today may mean being "without it" tomorrow. The case for the moral art of dreaming is infinitely more practical than many suppose. Moral effort frequently requires the exercise of imagination. To do good at all, we need some sense of what Goodness is and how our effort relates to some common Good. Without high motivation, even our best efforts can dissipate.

For myself, I am on the side of dreamers. You might expect no less from someone whose vocation is that of a preacher. Although I cannot quite say with George Bernard Shaw that "I was at home only in the realm of my imagination and at ease only with the mighty dead,"[11] I have some sense of what he meant. Individuals, societies, institutions, churches, nations, parties, books, programs, and policies will pass away; a good dream lasts forever.

And yet there is a case *against* dreams that should be recognized. In the first place, the art of dreaming rests upon an assumption that humankind *is capable* of moral improvement. And it is this assumption—to put it boldly, this *hope*—that has undergone much battering. The same 150 years which have seen the triumph of many a socially reforming movement have also seen great barbarity, inhumanity, and cruelty on a massive, hitherto undreamt-of, scale. Is it surprising if people who have lived through one or even two world wars, involving such crimes as Auschwitz, Belsen, Dresden, and Hiroshima, are a little weary of dreams? And even the generations who have grown up since the Second World War have lived with the terrifying possibility of all-out nuclear destruction. At worst, the pessimist has half the truth, even more. The political philosopher William Godwin has taught us how the phrase "all nature suffers" is no empty one. "Every animal, however minute, has a curious and subtle structure, rendering him susceptible, as it should seem, of piercing anguish. We cannot move a foot without becoming the means of destruction," he argues. But not only for animals, argues Godwin, is life frequently hellish:

> Let us survey the poor; oppressed, hungry, naked, denied all the gratifications of life, and all that nourishes the mind. They are either tormented with the injustice, or chilled into lethargy . . . Contemplate the physiognomy of the species. Observe the traces of stupidity, of low cunning, of rooted insolence, of withered hope, and narrow selfishness, where the characters of wisdom, independence and disinterestedness might have been inscribed. Reflect on the horrors of war, that last invention of deliberate profligacy for the misery of man. Think of the variety of wounds, the multiplication of anguish, the desolation of countries, towns destroyed, harvests flaming, inhabitants perishing by thousands of hunger and cold.

Who can deny the truth of Godwin's conclusion that "the whole history of the human species, taken in one point of view, appears a vast abortion?"[12] If, as Tolstoy once held, it is possible for humans to conspire together to do good, so too can they conspire (and how successfully) to do evil. The notion that we are fundamentally capable of moral regeneration may, to some, appear itself to be *the* dream—one, for which, as yet, evidence is still wanting.

In the second place, dreaming can become a compulsion, all demanding, all pervasive. Dreaming can become religion. And like all religion it can serve good or bad causes. To find oneself a part, however small, of the cause of moral good can be an uplifting, edifying experience. But if we are honest, we will know the ambiguity of the satisfaction that it gives to our souls. There is a beautiful incident in David Lewis's biography of Martin Luther King worth relating. It concerns a seventy-two-year-old black woman from Montgomery, Alabama, who got battered for refusing to ride on a segregated bus. She walked to work, almost fifty miles, and afterwards when asked how she felt, she replied, "My feets is tired but my soul is at rest."[13]

One morning at breakfast in the Linzey family, I recall waxing eloquent about dreams of a better world arising from my not inconsiderable, and, as it so happened, not unflattering mail. At the end of all my eloquence, my long-suffering wife spoke out: "I want you to know, Andrew, that there are two kinds of people in the world: saints and martyrs. Saints are the people who do good, and martyrs are the people who have to live with them."[14] How often I have reflected upon that thought and realized that not only animals need the movement for animal protection.

In the third place, the art of dreaming can so easily turn into a narrow, lifeless moralism. It happens something like this: Dreams raise people's hopes and expectations; they can motivate people to great heroic heights, but after a time they can also be a source of the most profound disappointment. Many humanitarians *are* disappointed people. It is this disappointment that can give rise to resentments, even hostility. I am reminded of the line from George Bernard Shaw: "I know many |blood| sportsmen; and none of them are ferocious. I know several humanitarians; and they are all ferocious."[15]

But the most worrying feature of the animal movement today is not its moral disappointment or even its ferocity, but its self-righteousness. What is most worrying is the way in which some of us have come to enjoy a good condemnation as others enjoy a good dinner.[16] Animal people have something to learn in this respect from the Christian tradition. For the Christian Church has for centuries excelled in self-righteousness. Christians have cajoled, intimidated, vilified, persecuted, imprisoned, tortured, burnt, and mutilated those who disagreed with them. There is hardly an implement of torture used in the world today that has not had an antecedent ecclesiastical use at one time or another. The Spanish Inquisition, I assure you, was no invention of pagan imagination. But what most of us have learnt—most, but I have to say, not all—is that, morality aside, it does not work. Hundreds of years of pagan persecution have not produced Christian civilization. Moral intimidation and self-righteousness do not make people good, or even better than they were.

This then is the debit side of dreaming—it can turn ordinary, sometimes callous, indifferent but otherwise well-meaning people into individuals so convinced of the moral rectitude of their own convictions that they become purists—indeed, so pure that almost everyone else is thought of as impure or unclean in relation to them.

In fact, however, there is no pure land on earth. We "all have sinned and fallen short of the glory of God."[17] I have been a vegetarian for thirty years, many of which I have spent trying to be a vegan. In practice this means not only abstaining from the primary products of slaughter (flesh, fish, and fowl) but also all the myriad by-products of animal exploitation. I have failed. The fact is that *all* vegans fail. It is simply not possible completely and absolutely to extricate oneself from all the by-products of animal exploitation. The non-leather shoes I am wearing have doubtless been tested for their toxicity on animals. Most postage stamps we lick in the world today consist of glue which comes from the offal which derives from the slaughterhouse. Ninety percent of beer contains dead animals. Fresh fruit is as a matter of course doused with insect or animal wax. There is hardly a human-made product—from fire-extinguisher substances to wall decorations—that has not at some point been the subject of animal tests.

This does not mean that we should not go on trying to avoid dependence upon animal products. But we must be clear that our Western society is so inextricably bound up with the exploitation of animals in almost every conceivable way that it is simply not possible for any one of us to claim that we are absolutely free from this exploitation, either through the food we eat, the products we buy, or indeed the taxes we pay. I do not say this to discourage any would-be fellow-traveler on the vegan road. By no means. But it is essential that all of us realize that there is no pure land. I see no grounds anywhere for self-righteousness, especially when it comes to our involvement with animals.[18] A clean conscience is a figment of the imagination or, as Schweitzer once put it, "an invention of the devil."[19]

Imagine another scene. It is another hot, sunny day. The date is April 4, 1969, just six years after Martin's speech in Washington. The place is the Lorraine Hotel in Memphis, Tennessee. Martin is staying here before he addresses one more civil rights meeting. The time is about six o'clock. He goes out on to the balcony to take some air. Less than three minutes later, he is shot. The assassin escapes. A crowd gathers. Martin is dead on arrival at the hospital.

Imagine yet another scene. The date is July 16, 1837—just thirteen years after the London meeting which founded the RSPCA. The place is Birmingham, England; a cemetery, to be precise. Somewhere in this place lies the body of Arthur Broome. A burial place, unmarked, unloved, uncared for. The Society whose work came into existence as a result of his vision forgot about him. The man who changed the world for animals died in obscurity and oblivion. According to historians, "he seems to have slipped out of the world unwept, unhonored, and unsung."[20]

True dreaming involves real cost. It is that openness to bear the cost of dreaming that makes dreamers the people they are. Anyone can entertain hopes of social progress; only the dreamer lays his or her life on the line. Dreams can truly become more important than life itself. And truly the stuff of dreams, as well as nourishing our soul, can give us life.

Today the animal movement is more split than ever between "dreamers" and "realists"; between those who want "pie in the sky," as it is sometimes called, and others who insist upon the necessity—if you will forgive the meaty analogy—of "ham where we am." Should we aim for the abolition of all animal experiments or focus on only some? Should we oppose all zoos or the most inhumane ones? Should we be working toward humane slaughter or no slaughter? Should we campaign against all trapping or trapping solely for commercial purposes? The list goes on, and so do the arguments and the debates. Now I do not want to suggest that these debates are unimportant. On the contrary, they represent fundamental divisions within the movement— and most people know where I stand in relation to them. But what I want to suggest is that the dreamer and the realist need each other. There is an ugly polarity developing within our movement which, I believe, is not only counter-productive but actually unnecessary. The simple truth is we need to match our ability to dream with our determination to realize our dreams. "I am, in-deed, a practical dreamer," wrote Mahatma Gandhi. "My dreams are not airy nothings. I want to convert my dreams into realities, as far as possible."[21] It is this spirit of *practical dreaming*, so char-acteristic of our visionary forebears, that I want to commend to you.

There is no more pressing task than the making of our dream both practicable and intelligible. And what is our dream? It is a dream deeply embedded within the Judeo-Christian tradition. It is a dream still capable of stirring the imagination and strength-ening our will. It is nothing less than a dream of peace; of a time when, according to Isaiah:

> The wolf shall dwell with the lamb,
>   and the leopard shall lie down with the kid,
> and the calf and the lion and the fatling together,
>   and a little child shall lead them.
> The cow and the bear shall feed;
>   their young shall lie down together;
>   and the lion shall eat straw like the ox.
> The suckling child shall play over the hole of the asp,
>   and the weaned child shall put his hand on the adder's
>   den.
> They shall not hurt or destroy
>   in all my holy mountain;
> for the earth shall be full of the knowledge of the
>   LORD
>   as the waters cover the sea.[22]

This then is the vision of peace—not only between humans and animals but also between animals themselves. What the biblical writers are expressing here—and in the other important pas-sages in Genesis, Hosea, Jeremiah, Amos, Psalms, Colossians, Romans, Ephesians, and Revelation[23]—is the conviction that or-der and harmony and peace is God's original will for creation.

Imagine then a different world: A world of peaceful coexistence between all species. A world where there is room for all, and every need is met. A world teeming with life, with each creature living free of violence. A world in which human beings self-evidently reflect the glory and love of God. A world in which humans look after the world, knowing it to be God's own possession and therefore a sacred treasure. A world in which everything is blessed, and its very life is a blessing to God. A world transfigured by Sabbath thanksgiving, where humans precede other creatures only in grateful, reverential praise and worship. A world in which all creatures, animate and inanimate, sentient and nonsentient, human and nonhuman, exist in perfect unity before their Creator.

This world is none other than that described in Genesis, chapter one. God creates all life, giving the earth to be shared among all forms of life (vv. 10–25). Humans are made in God's image and given the commission to have dominion (vv. 26–28). However, dominion means not tyranny but responsibility. Finally, humans are commanded, along with the animals, to be vegetarian, to live free of violence (vv. 29–30). Because of this, God "saw everything he had made, and behold it was very good" (v. 31). Genesis chapter one may not be so much a statement of *what was*, but *what is yet to be*.

This then, as I see it, is our dream. It provides us with both a challenge and an invitation.

First, the challenge. There are people today who say that these dreams are things of the past, that they represent wanton anticipation at best, or, at worst, reckless fantasy. There are those who say we should give up altogether on cosmic dreams and concentrate solely on the narrow, self-serving gains we can make in the short span between our life and our certain death. There are people who despair totally and absolutely of any approximation of these dreams, or of their capacity to give hope, or of the human capacity to realize them. And yet who is the realist here? At the end of the day (and our day's end may well be sooner than we think) our clever—but visionless—technological accomplishments have brought us to the brink of total destruction. Our challenge is to insist that living peaceably, developing every ounce of humanity left within us, is not just a moral extra, but actually essential to the survival of our own species and every species. Living humanely is not now, if it has ever been, an optional extra. Everything hangs now on whether human beings can become more human. The protection of the natural world is the surest way of securing human survival. Perhaps unless we can share the earth, we will have nothing to share.

The pioneers of our movement sought to change the moral feeling of the countries in which they worked. That aim remains our challenge, and it is a challenge that has to be made repeatedly to institutions, corporations, societies, governments, businesses, multinationals, schools, colleges, universities, and—not least of all—the churches. I will not mince my words here. The Christian Church is the proud possessor of a dream which it has itself only faintly grasped, frequently misunderstood, and all too often practically frustrated. Buried somewhere in the archives of the ASPCA lies an unpublished history of the American society written by Edward Buffet. His chapter on "Ecclesiastical Relations" begins as follows:

> The aloofness of the clergy, with some exceptions, from active concern for animal welfare work is a perennial subject of remark amongst humanitarians. One can conjecture various explanations, but none of them is wholly convincing. Their apathy can sometimes be overcome by personal contact. Most of the ministers are good at heart, but they have some mental twist which needs to be straightened out. It still remains that there is something in their profession which forms a hindrance, rather than a help, to acquiring that sympathetic imagination which conditions pity for suffering animals. That this is an inversion of the true influence of Christianity, goes without saying. The result is to produce bitterness against official religion in humane workers generally, even in those who are religious people themselves, and we find an occasional humanely-minded preacher excoriating the apathy of his brother clergy.[24]

These lines were written in 1924. More than seventy-five years later it is astonishing, as well as lamentable, to see how little has changed. It is important to appreciate that the failure of the Church in this regard is not just a failure to take on another moral cause in the world. Always the Church is asked to be involved in one cause, campaign, reform movement or another—and understandably so. But the failure of the Church is not just that kind of failure, important though that might be. Neither is it, I suggest, simply a failure on the part of the clergy who have, as Buffet suggests, some disposition toward "mental twists" in their thinking. That may or may not be so, of course, though I sometimes have sympathy for people who feel that those who want to be ordained nowadays cannot be quite right in the head. Neither do I think that the failure of the Church is due overmuch to the moral apathy of my brother and sister clergy. In general, I find them, if anything, overeager to moralize—even condemn—and, on some issues, I rather think the Church has done too much condemning with too little actual understanding. No, I suggest that the failure of the Church to champion humaneness is a fundamental failure on its own part to understand its own Gospel. For that Gospel as exemplified in Jesus Christ is about service to the sick, poor, disadvantaged, diseased, imprisoned, and all others who are regarded as the lowest of all, and not least to the whole world of suffering nonhuman creatures, too. There is no theological reason sufficient to prevent Christian concern for animals, and many, many theological reasons why such concern should now be viewed as a priority. For too long Christian churches have been part of the problem rather than part of the solution. We cannot love God and be indifferent to suffering creatures.

It is time then for the challenge to be posed to the Church directly—not only to the churches, of course, and certainly not because they are some of the best institutions, but rather because they are some of the worst. We need in this movement not just Christians but those of every philosophical persuasion or none. But let us be quite clear: Whoever else is in this movement, it is time for the churches—with their immense power and human resources—to throw themselves into the making of a more humane world. We must say to the churches not "Here is another moral cause, please back it" but rather "This cause is *your* cause, and if you are to have any credible claim to be part of the Gospel of love, your place must be alongside us." And I believe that when this challenge is made, as it is increasingly being made, churches have no alternative but to be involved in a little heart-searching and no

little repentance. Already there are some signs in the recent pronouncements of Anglican archbishops, in Papal Encyclicals, and
in one report to the World Council of Churches in particular that
our challenge is being heard and, in at least some cases, met.[25]
What our movement has failed to do, however, is to make the theological challenge direct and in the theological language that the
churches understand. For myself, I am determined, as my life's
work, to ensure that this theological tradition gives heed to the
plight of animals not just as an issue of sentiment or feeling but
as a matter of reason and justice. The animals deserve no less.

I want now to turn from challenge to invitation. Desirable
though it is, social challenge is not enough. In addition our task
has to be to invite individuals to begin taking steps, however fal-
teringly, toward progressive disengagement from inhumanity to
animals. Here there is much to be done, and much already being
done. Scientists must be encouraged to use alternatives to animals in research. Entertainers must be encouraged to think twice
before using animals in their films, television programs, and especially their advertisements. All of us need to be invited to buy
products free from cruelty. All of us need to find ways of eating
free of violence. All of us need to become conscientious consumers, testing the power of our dreams in the supermarket.

The challenge to us is how we can encourage individuals as
consumers, as parents, as educators, as ministers, as lawyers, as
businesspeople, as senators to take some steps, however apparently small and insignificant, toward the realization of our dream.
"Making peace with creation"; after years of wanton violence and
cruelty, it makes a good line. But we have to commend our
dreams, and invite individual response without intimidation,
without moralism, without self-righteousness, without violence,
without pretending that there is a pure land and that we alone in-
habit it. Neither do we all have to be agreed on precisely the same
programs or the same priorities. Here, as everywhere, there is legitimate room for debate, disagreement, and dissent. But one
thing is essential—that we give each other hope, that we avoid
rancor, jealousy, and acrimony. There is a line, I think from T. S.
Eliot, which goes something like this: "When mankind is moving
in the wrong direction, the man going the right way will appear, at

first, to be lost." I never cease to be impressed by the dedication and professionalism of many individuals working, often at great expense, and frequently under great hardship, and more often than not in the face of outrageous criticism, to accomplish humane goals. Anyone who begins to set his or her foot on the road to recovering a sense of humanity and justice in our dealings with animals begins to pay a price. We must find ways of encouraging one another, whatever immediate strategies or principles divide us. It is fair to remind ourselves that it is not animals alone that should benefit from the increase in humanity.

Martin Luther King, in an uncanny, prophetic-like speech in Memphis shortly before his death, uttered these words:

> Well, I don't know what will happen now. We've got some difficult days ahead. But it doesn't matter with me now, because I've been to the mountaintop . . . I just want to do God's will. And He's allowed me to go up to the mountain, and I've looked over, and I've seen the promised land. I may not get there with you. But I want you to know tonight, that we, as a people will get to the promised land.[26]

Like Martin Luther King, we know that we have some difficult days ahead. We know that we do not know "what will happen now." And yet we may also sense—even if we have not been to the mountaintop—that there is a future for our dreams. On Martin's tombstone are inscribed the following words: "Free at last, free at last, thank God Almighty, I am free at last." The suffering animals of the world are not yet free from human cruelty. And neither are we yet free to live in the world of our dreams, except perhaps in our imaginations. But, to borrow the words of an old, black slave: "We ain't what we ought to be, and we ain't what we want to be, and we ain't what we're going to be. But thank God, we ain't what we was."[27]

10

Moral Means
to Moral Ends

In the previous chapter I sought to describe the Christian vision of universal peace and the need for us to commit ourselves to a program of progressive disengagement from injury to animals. But if the goal is peace, then that goal must dictate the means, and one means that cannot logically be utilized is that of violence. For me this is not just a question of strategy, although I certainly do think that violent strategies are practically counter-productive. It is rather a question of internal consistency. It is plainly contradictory to pursue the vision of a more peaceful world by violent means. In this chapter, I try to spell out the nature of the contradiction and why it is imperative for animal advocates to reject unambiguously all forms of violent struggle.

Oxford has seen a series of bomb attacks on commercial businesses and on at least one scientist. Who precisely is responsible for these activities seems unclear. In the case of the attacks on fur, leather, and woolen businesses in Oxford, to my knowledge no animal group has claimed responsibility.

Since we do not know who is responsible, we must question the automatic assumption that animal-rights activists are to blame. There is the famous case in the United States of one commercial animal concern apparently engaging an *agent provocateur* to inspire terrorist acts against its own company. Since the PR fallout is so obviously hostile to animal-rights activism, one cannot always be sure who is planting the bomb, and under whose tutelage, and for precisely what purpose. However wistful it may appear, we do well to think beyond the banner headlines. Who, for example, would have believed that people acting for the French intelligence service were responsible for blowing up the Greenpeace boat *Rainbow Warrior*?

Nevertheless, if we believe the reports, it seems generally indisputable that animal-rights activists are using bombs to advance their cause. It is not difficult to understand the desperation that leads to such violence. Animals have been, and still are, treated with hideous cruelty around the world. Most human beings look upon animals as things to be eaten. Historically, animals have been defined as little more than things: resources, tools, units of production, objects of entertainment, and simply as means to human ends. Our use of animals has only just begun to receive the ethical attention it deserves.

Moreover, it is unwise to be innocent about the realities of power. Those who wish to exploit animals for food and for science—to take only two examples—have every conceivable means at their disposal: powerful multinationals, government funding, mostly sympathetic media, not to mention sheer human self-interest. Cosmetic companies in the United States decided in one year alone to spend $8.5 million on anti-antivivisection activities.[1] Unsurprisingly, those who try to speak up for animals can justifiably feel a little outclassed by the strength of the status quo. In the light of this—and much more one could document—is it surprising that some advocates are prone to commit acts that they know will receive media attention and provoke public awareness?

I am not enough of an historian to know how far, if at all, violence or militancy, or both, have been essential accompaniments to fundamental social change. I want to think that moral conflict can be managed without acrimony or malice and most of all without violence and terror; but historians of social change may laugh at my naivety.

Historical speculation apart, there are two strong internal reasons why animal rightists—of all social campaigners—cannot support violence without loss of intellectual integrity. Animal-rights theory is obviously indebted to the notion of rights. To curtail philosophical discussion at this point, we may define a right as a fundamental moral limit—a limit to be exceeded, if at all, only under the most extreme circumstances or, most usually in animal-rights theory, only when the individual concerned may be improved by it. Hence animal rightists oppose animal experimentation on the grounds that it is wrong to use one individual sentient creature simply in the service of another. To use such a being without its consent as a means to another's end is to treat it unjustly.[2]

But if that is correct, and I'm inclined to think it is, animal rightists must logically oppose the use or treatment of some humans in ways that are similarly unjust. If it is unjust to infringe an animal's right to be spared suffering (save when it is in its own individual interest), so it also must be wrong to inflict suffering on humans (also sentient subjects). It should be obvious that, for example, to fire-bomb a shop renders the individual human concerned, directly or indirectly, liable to harm.

True, no human, to my knowledge, has yet been seriously harmed or killed, but that may be more a matter of luck than anything else. Fire-bombing is inherently indiscriminate. For whatever end, the rights of one or more individual human beings have been put at risk. Animal-rights theory, at least that based on the most philosophically developed position, must necessarily eschew such infringement of individual rights—animal or human. It must be as wrong to fire-bomb a fur shop as it is to inflict suffering on animals in pursuit of scientific advantage. To pursue animal rights by infringing human rights is logically self-contradictory.

The reply may come that it is justifiable in utilitarian terms to balance one evil against another, and hence choose the lesser evil, which may or may not justify specific targets where the risk to individual humans is minimal.[3] While it may be possible for thoroughgoing utilitarians to hold this view, rights theorists are precluded from doing so. This is because the characteristic thrust of rights theory, in contrast to utilitarianism, consists in its rejection of consequences as an adequate basis for ethics. According to rights theory, the justifiability of animal experiments, to take one example, cannot be determined by appeals to consequences alone. The issue, sharply put, is not whether we gain from animal experiments but rather whether they are ill-gotten gains. Again, it must be as wrong to fire-bomb shops, which may injure humans (or animals), in pursuit of animal rights as it is to use laboratory animals for the sake of some greater human advantage.

What then should be most worrying to those who adhere to animal-rights theory is that those activists who fire-bomb shops apparently rely on the same kind of moral justification most frequently used by those who justify violence to animals. Those of us who are sympathetic to animal rights must unambiguously oppose violence—in all its forms—even, and especially, when it is perpetrated by animal-rights activists themselves.

Although the question of moral self-contradiction is paramount, there are also good grounds for regarding violent strategies as counter-productive. While activists are right to see public discussion, fueled by the media, as a precondition of social change, trusting the contemporary media is a hazardous exercise. Activists who take to violence provide copy for the media, which are both eager to report violence and also, at the same time, to brand movements wholesale as "terrorist."

The general knock-on effect is incalculable: All those who work for the humane treatment of animals become suspect. The great swathe of popular opinion sympathetic to anti-cruelty work becomes alienated or hostile. Those who have long argued that concern for animals is anti-human are given empirical proof. The stereotype is confirmed: Thoroughgoing ethical concern for animals is abnormal, even fanatical.

There is one other consideration perhaps more important than all else: Any responsible animal-rights strategy must, to some degree, embrace gradualism. Realistically, while significant advances and improvements for animals are possible worldwide during the next century, the world is not going to turn vegan overnight. This seems an obvious truth, and yet some animal-rights rhetoric recklessly exaggerates the rate and possibility of social change.

Although some vegans will dislike me for saying it, the purism which some of them want the human race to enjoin presupposes the very stuff of heaven. I once saw a poster with the slogan, "If you're not a vegan—you're a Nazi." Such slogans are not only inaccurate, they are dangerous. Most dangerous of all is the mistaken assumption that there is a "pure" land or that there are "pure" people.

Given that there is no "pure" land possible on earth, animal rightists need to match their vision of a new world for animals with a tenacious commitment to gradual, pragmatic, democratic change. I used to think that nonviolent civil disobedience—after the style of Martin Luther King—might provide a way forward for those seeking fundamental change. But I do not even *think* that now, and for three main reasons. The first is that a sizeable amount of animal activism either constitutes violence or leads to violence. The range and rate of activist law-breaking is indiscriminate: sending hoax bombs, senseless destruction of property, trashing labs, and the harassment of individuals. But the Christian Gospel eschews violence. Violence—in all its forms—is part of the problem, not part of the solution.

Second, I do not accept the despair sometimes articulated by activists to the effect that the governmental system will always fail the animals. Of course governments can and do fail the cause of animals, but in a democracy (however imperfect) the possibility of lawful, peaceful change is always an option. For example, the UK has elected a government with the most progressive range of policies on animal welfare ever presented to the public by a mainstream political party.[4] In a democracy, criminal tactics are an attempt to shortcut the system.

Third, moral ends can only properly and fully be achieved by moral means. One of the lines of Martin Luther King that used to impress me was this: "We cannot in all good conscience obey your unjust laws and abide by your unjust system, because non-cooperation with evil is as much a moral obligation as is cooperation with good . . ."[5] This is fine rhetoric (and none the worse for that), but it cannot be easily translated to the struggle for animal rights. Since animal exploitation is endemic in society, a logical and thoroughgoing policy of civil disobedience would entail an almost constant state of conscientious law-breaking—in short, a war waging on almost all established law. I cannot believe that this is a serious option.

To pursue moral means requires that we reject strategies of

blatant manipulation and intimidation. Not to do so risks not a decrease but an increase in the total amount of moral evil in the world today. It assumes what is even empirically false, namely that there are unambiguously good and unambiguously evil people—whereas in fact what needs to be perceived is our *common* complicity in animal exploitation.

People will not be easily cajoled, intimidated, threatened, or bludgeoned beyond their moral senses into a new world; they need to be rationally persuaded. The only viable strategy is to lay before them the vision of living peaceably with animals, arguing for its rational foundations, and encouraging individuals to take one step after another along the road to a less exploitative world. As I see it, there really is no alternative to the strategy already advanced: progressive personal and social disengagement from injury to animals.

11

Toward
Cruelty-free
Science

Even among those who are sympathetic to animals there is a significant number who believe that harmful experiments upon animals can be justified as long as humans benefit. "Surely something must be done to prevent the spread of human disease?" they ask, and the assumption always is that experimentation as a method will help the weak and vulnerable human beings who have to suffer. In this chapter, I explain why such an assumption cannot be properly made—indeed, flies in the face of actual evidence. In the history of experimentation we have concrete evidence that the causes of preventing human suffering and preventing animal suffering are not two causes but *one and the same cause*. In conclusion, I also show how the argument for choice, if valid, justifies the extension of ethical choice to all those who wish to disengage themselves from animal cruelty.

Imagine a scene in your mind: Experimental subjects are receiving diagnostic tests for tuberculosis. One test requires the instillation of tuberculin solution in the eye, another the injection of tuberculin into the muscle, and the third a test injection of tuberculin into the skin. One hundred and sixty subjects are selected. The published report describes the discomforts and injuries resulting from the eye test, including "a decidedly uncomfortable lesion" and "serious inflammation of the eye." One observer described the plight of the experimental subjects as follows: "[they] would lie in their beds moaning all night from the pain in their eyes." Also, "They kept their little hands pressed over their eyes, unable to sleep from the sensations they had to undergo."

These experiments were performed in 1908 by doctors and associates of the William Pepper Clinical Laboratory of the University of Pennsylvania. The experimental victims, however, were not animals but humans—children to be precise. In fact 160 orphans, all but twenty-six of whom resided in the St. Vincent's Home for Orphans, a Catholic orphanage in Philadelphia.

Imagine now another picture in your mind. It is a pamphlet published by the New York Anti-Vivisection Society in 1915. It details (among other things) the inoculation of consumptive germs, the deliberate injection of syphilis, and the grafting on of malignant cancers. This publication is not concerned with animal experimentation, however. The title of this pamphlet is not *Animal Vivisection*—but *Human Vivisection*, and the experiments it describes are performed not on animal subjects but human ones, mostly children to be precise.

These examples are not products of my imagination. Both come from a remarkable new book titled *Subjected to Science*, with the subtitle *Human Experimentation in America before the Second World War*. It is written by Susan E. Lederer, who is associate professor of the humanities at the Hershey Medical Center at Penn State University, and published by the Johns Hopkins University Press.[1] It is clear from the book that Lederer is not herself an anti-vivisectionist, and indeed she is not wholly unfavorable to both experimentation on humans as well as animal subjects.

All the more remarkable then that one of her principal claims is, "During this period [before the Second World War], the moral issues raised by experimenting on human beings were most intensely pursued by men and women committed to the protection of animals. Already devoted to saving dogs, cats and other animals from the vivisector's knife, anti-vivisectionists warned that the replacement of the family physician by the 'scientists at the bedside' would inspire non-therapeutic experimentation on vulnerable human beings." Also, "Human vivisection must be understood in the larger context of animal protection."[2] Not only are these claims made in this book, but they are also amply documented. The truth of the matter is that the campaign against human experimentation was spearheaded by anti-vivisectionists.

I will spare you some of the gruesome details, except one which is too revealing to be omitted. In 1931, one scientist, W. Osler Abbott, performed intubing and X-ray experiments on human subjects. Lederer notes that "Abbott ended up with a roster of subjects, young and old, white and black, male and female, although he noted that his 'clientele' eventually dwindled down to large, older women, the human counterpart, he said, of the 'big, lazy, overweight bitch (from the animal house) that could be counted upon to lie down and wag her tail while being worked over.'" And Lederer further comments, "That investigators would treat human subjects like laboratory animals was precisely what anti-vivisectionists feared."[3]

I foray into this little history because it totally demolishes the claim still heard from the mouths of vivisectors that we must experiment on animals because we cannot experiment on humans. The truth is that not only animals but a whole range of defenseless human subjects have been subject to scientific experiments for well over a century. The same century that has seen an explosion of experiments on animals has also witnessed experiments on almost every conceivable kind of vulnerable human subject: not only children and orphans but also Jews, blacks, prisoners of war, the mentally unwell, unconsenting soldiers, and invalids. And to complete the list we must now add (in the UK) the legalization of experiments on embryos up to fourteen days old. Those who think that vivisectors are friends of the vulnerable are deceiving themselves.

To those who mouth the wholly misleading view that we must choose between "your dog or your baby," we must repeat the entirely truthful counter-claim made by early anti-vivisectionists: It is not a choice between "your dog or your baby" but rather "your dog AND your baby."[4]

Right from the start, anti-vivisectionists have claimed that the logic of experimentation, if morally valid, equally applies to human subjects as well. Nowhere in human history has such a claim been more well justified and well documented. Recall, for example, the view of Lewis Carroll who, as early as 1875 when the practice of vivisection was just beginning at Oxford, reserved his greatest mockery for the idea that vivisection would never be extended to include human subjects.[5]

C. S. Lewis, too, in a remarkably adroit paper on vivisection published in 1947, prophezied that, ". . . no argument for experiments on animals can be found which is not also an argument for experiments on inferior men. If we cut up beasts simply because they cannot prevent us and because we are backing up our own side in the struggle for existence, it is only logical to cut up imbeciles, criminals, enemies, or capitalists for the same reason. Indeed experiments on men have already begun. We all hear that Nazi scientists have done them. We all suspect that our own scientists may begin to do so, in secret, at any moment."[6]

What Carroll and Lewis and many others in the antivivisection movement have seen is that human liberation and animal liberation are one and the same cause. The argument for benefit that justifies animal experimentation also justifies experimentation on human subjects. Indeed the logic of our position is accepted even by those who oppose it. In the words of the philosopher Raymond Frey, "If securing the benefit licenses (painful) experiments on animals, it equally licenses (painful) experiments on humans."[7] In my view we must oppose totally and absolutely the idea that utility, benefit, can in itself justify the infliction of harm on innocents. The only obvious exception to this principle is where the infliction of harm is for *the individual's own interest* in, for example, a medical or veterinary operation. Most people are of course horrified by the idea that we should nowadays experiment on children. But if we ask *why* such experimentation is so morally abhorrent, the answer is surely that children are vulnerable, unprotected, undefended, weak, they cannot give their consent, and, most important of all, they are morally innocent. But notice how these things are true equally not only of children but also of weak, undefended, unprotected, vulnerable, and morally innocent animals. I will not hide my basic conviction that the infliction of suffering on innocent, defenseless beings, human or animal, is nothing less than intrinsically evil.

If we are to have ethical science, then it must be a science that recognizes certain moral constraints. Not everything that could be done, should be done. Slowly but surely we have begun to see

that there must be moral constraints in relation to human subjects. In the words of the Helsinki Declaration adopted by the
World Medical Assembly in 1964, based on the Nuremberg Code
of 1947, ". . . concern for the interests of the subject must always
prevail over the interest of science and society."[8] This admirable
principle must now be applied to all experimental subjects
whether human or animal.

Nowadays, however, experimentation is justified not only on the
basis that we have the right to benefit the human species at whatever cost to animals, but also on the basis that humans have the
right to choose. Recently, during a radio discussion on the ethics of
xenografts (pig to human transplants), I was asked: "What right
have you to deny this choice to somebody else?" Choice has become the new god in moral debate. The criterion of morality is not
now whether something is good or bad, right or wrong in itself, but
rather how far it prevents someone else doing something regard-
less of whether that something is in itself either right or wrong.

Hence experiments on animals are now justified on the basis
that people have the right to choose the medical treatments they
want—even costly, complex, and risky treatments like animal to
human transplants. But if choice is to be the criterion for medical practice, what of the right of those who *do not* want animal
transplants or any medicine based on animal exploitation?

Currently it is almost impossible to obtain any medicine that
has not been tested on animals. But the health service ought to
take account of those who do not want animal-based treatments
and who reject—on conscientious and ethical grounds—our exploitation of animals. The right to choose, if valid, should now be
extended to those who want medical treatment without animal
suffering. This simple idea is potentially revolutionary in its effects. After all, anti-vivisectionists also pay taxes but as it stands
they are *denied their right* to choose.

To those who say "We have the right to choose," we should say
"We also have the right of ethical choice." Just think of it: the right
to consult medical practitioners who oppose vivisection, the
right to treatments not based on animal exploitation, the right to
medical care from those who hold our ethical view that all sentient creatures should be treated with respect.

If we are to embrace a new pluralistic world where no absolutes of right and wrong hold sway, then here is an opportunity for anti-vivisectionists to ensure that their choice is fully recognized and properly funded. In capitalist societies, we have great power as consumers, taxpayers, and patients. Twenty years ago, if you wrote to cosmetics manufacturers to protest cosmetics tests on animals, you would have been told that human health required them. Now, after generations of protests and many thousands of such letters, cosmetics manufacturers are only too eager to tell you that they are phasing out such experiments, or that they are now funding alternatives, or even in some cases that they have given up such testing altogether. Indeed, since November 1997, all animal testing for finished cosmetic products has now ceased in the United Kingdom.[9]

I say that this idea is "revolutionary" because while there will always be some humans who want to live at the expense of other creatures, there are large numbers who want to embrace a genuinely ethical lifestyle. According to an animal welfare poll conducted by MORI in the United Kingdom, fifty percent of people disapproved of drug testing on animals, and a massive seventy-seven percent were opposed to cosmetic testing on animals.[10] Just think: Half of the British population oppose the most mainstream use of animals in experiments today. Now is the time to turn this moral conviction into practical politics—by demanding ethical medicine for those who oppose harmful experiments. Ignorance keeps vivisection in business. The harm and cruelty inflicted is by and large invisible. Our challenge must be to make it visible, to provide the essential information that will allow people to make an informed ethical choice. If only fifty percent of all the funding and resources that currently go into orthodox medical research, pharmaceutical companies, and drug-based therapies went into alternatives and ethically based treatments, what a different world it would be both for animals and for us.

Some of you may be tempted to think some of this rather visionary, but I ask you to bear in mind that we are already witnessing a revolutionary change in our attitudes toward animals. Our ideas about animals are slowly but surely changing: The old idea that animals are simply resources, commodities, laboratory tools, models, things here for our use, is giving way to another idea that animals as sentient beings have intrinsic value, dignity, and rights. We are changing the world for animals by changing people's ideas about the world and the place of animals within it.

Experimental science for over a century has pursued its tasks at the expense of the innocent, and it has assumed that human interests narrowly conceived should always be paramount no matter the costs to the victims. But even among scientists there is a growing sense that inflicting harm is unfortunate, disagreeable, even a necessary evil. All this stems, at least in part, from a new perception of what human beings are and what it means to be human. In the words of C. S. Lewis, "Our superiority ought to consist at least in part in not behaving like a vivisector."[11] There is a new sensitivity that humanity can no longer justify the advancement of its interests at the expense of the rest of creation, and an abhorrence at the infliction of harm, pain, and suffering on other creatures.

Those early anti-vivisectionists who campaigned against human as well as animal vivisection have been proved right: A world in which cruelty to animals goes unchecked is bound to be a morally unsafe world for human beings.

Brave New
Unnatural World

On some issues Christians have provided a strong prophetic witness. Historically, one thinks of William Wilberforce's fight against the slave trade and Lord Shaftesbury's campaign against the exploitation of children in factories. More recently, one thinks of Martin Luther King's crusade for civil rights and Archbishop Desmond Tutu's struggle against racism and apartheid. But there are other issues of justice where Christians speak with conflicting voices, and some issues where a Christian conscience has found hardly any voice at all. One of those issues where Christians have yet to register anything like the appropriate level of concern is over the genetic manipulation of life.

Despite fashionable talk of the "integrity of creation," when it comes to confronting precisely the issue of how far we should go in redesigning the structure of life itself, Christian voices, more often than not, grow silent. This silence indicates a vacuum in moral theology that can only be explained by the history of neglect when it comes to basic issues that should affect our understanding of animals as God's creatures. In this chapter, I appeal to our imaginations in the hope of rekindling a need for a kind of theological "back to basics."

Imagine that you are sitting at a table with a large electronic button in the middle of it. Imagine that this button is connected to all species of animal and plant life. Once pressed, it will unleash forces that will enable you to restructure and redesign all life on this planet.

Animals and plants will be redesigned into objects for our

convenience. Pigs will have human genes injected into them to make them grow faster; hairless pigs will be designed for consumer acceptability; cows will conveniently quadruple their capacity for milk; featherless chickens will be designed especially for intensive conditions in hot climates—animals tailor-made to the demands of our stomachs; animals genetically modified for our taste and convenience.

Will you press this button? Will you by this one act genetically redesign the nature of animal life? I hope that at least some would share with me a sense that this would be going too far, that such a step would *really* infringe the integrity of creation and reduce sentient life to the status of objects and things.

But I have to say that something like this button has already been pressed and is being pressed daily. And the means through which such control is being exercised is the science of genetic engineering. Research units worldwide are pioneering ways in which we can secure absolute genetic control over other creatures. The control of DNA, the very structure of life, is now within our grasp. And the examples I gave of human DNA in pigs, cows as milk machines, and hairless pigs are already a possibility, if not a fact.[1] Images of science fiction are already becoming science fact.

Indeed, I have been brought face to face with one of these new scientific marvels. I went to Israel with the BBC to film the results of the genetic modification of poultry.[2] We visited a scientist who had redesigned chickens so that they had less plumage. The purpose? Apparently thinly feathered birds are less prone to heat stress and can therefore be reared in intensive conditions in hot climates. When pressed during the interview how he viewed these creatures, his reply was as frank as it was revealing: Animals reared for meat are economic commodities, "meat machines."

But, it may be said, what's new? Haven't we always exploited other creatures—not least of all through selective breeding? It is certainly not new that we are seeking to manipulate animal life, even in especially cruel ways. Indeed we must be clear that the selective breeding of farm animals already causes them suffering. The quest for "higher efficiency" means that animals are bred for faster growth rates. In practice this means risking the welfare of animals for profit. Examples include painful joint and leg problems in pigs, heart disease in broiler chickens, leg problems in beef cattle, and turkeys who cannot mate since their "body shape makes it impossible for their reproductive organs to come into contact." Apparently, turkeys have been "selected for huge meaty and profitable breasts, which make mounting impossible."[3]

No, it is not new that we are exploiting animals in new and cruel ways. But what is new is that we now have the absolute technological ability to reduce animals to things. Genetic engineering is one more step—yes—but also the ultimate step toward total human mastery over the animal world.

Patenting animals has become the commercial symbol of this new kind of relationship. For many years, researchers have used animals in laboratory tests, including cancer research. Many of these tests involve the artificial creation of cancer in animals. With this new technology at our disposal, we have been able to manipulate animals genetically so that they "naturally" develop cancer without human intervention. These self-creating laboratory tools—for that is what they are—are now actually patented in European law.

Patenting means that they are classified alongside other commodities, like new gadgets or consumer durables, as human inventions. The "oncomouse" (the name of the first patented animal) will ineluctably be followed by the oncopig, the oncochicken, and the oncochimp. Patenting utterly reduces the status of animals to things. Its purpose is to enable commercial enterprises to legally own their invention and to make a profit out of it. "It may be no exaggeration to say that we stand on the brink of a wholly new relationship to other creatures: no longer custodians of our fellow creatures but rather dealers in new commodities."[4]

To all these developments we can talk as much as we like about ethics committees and regulatory legislation and posses of inspectors (all of course may be welcome), but none of this is going to fundamentally thwart the forward thrust of this research—so long as we have the same basic idea of animals as resources. In order to think imaginatively, we have to think fundamentally; we have to address the underlying philosophic conception of animal life. We have to dig deeper to the theological bottom line, and that bottom line is this: We do not own animals; they do not belong to us.

As already noted, in some ways we Christians have only ourselves to blame, for we have allowed our ancient texts, like Genesis, to be interpreted as justifying might is right. Dominion means responsibility—that we have a divine duty to care for the earth—but so often we have been silent when others (including Christians themselves) have taken it to mean that the world is ours and we can do as we like with it.

The fundamental truth then is that it is not our world; it is God's world. We are set over it—not as masters—but as stewards and servants of God's moral purpose. Our vocation is to care, to tread softly on this earth, remembering that it does not belong to us. For myself, I recoil in horror at the prospect of ever-increasing human manipulation, control, and domination of the earth. The created world is not perfect, but it does have its own integrity and worth which compels respect. Our species more than ever suffers from an overdose of hubris, pride, the perpetual sin of thinking more highly of ourselves than we should, even that we are the only species that matters before God. Scientists are changing the doctrine of human sinfulness into the doctrine of human perfectibility. Who are we to make a world in which each and every species of life has no other reason for living except that of serving the advantage and comfort and convenience of the human species?

I do not believe overmuch in conspiracies by scientists, even conspiracies by politicians. The truth about genetic engineering is altogether more simple—and sinister. Genetic engineering is simply the practical outworking of a worldview that has abandoned any notion of God the Creator. No integrity of creation. No moral limits to the exploitation of creation. Indeed the very notion that there is something called "creation," or even "nature," worthy of respect, is itself being jettisoned.

I began by asking you to imagine pressing the button that would unleash the genetic engineering of animals. Imagine now that you sit in front of another table, with another electronic button before you. This device is connected not to animal life but to human life. Suppose that the pressing of this button would unleash the genetic manipulation of humans—suppose that by this one act you could genetically modify the antisocial behavior of the entire human race. Think about it: no vandalism, no alcoholism, no wife-beating, no child molestation, no rape, no social violence. With one act you could redesign the human species.

We are not, even here, so far away from the bounds of possibility as might be supposed. Given ten, twenty, thirty, forty, fifty years we shall have mapped all the genes—social, psychological, political, even perhaps spiritual—that make us who we are. When this happens, it cannot be long before social policy discourages the birth of certain humans with "high risk" genetic traits.

The two writers who have, in their differing ways, most understood the implications of genetic science applied to human society have been Aldous Huxley and C. S. Lewis. It was Huxley of course whose *Brave New World*, published in 1932, offered us the bleak prospect of totalitarian social control of human reproduction. Whether his book was, in the words of one commentator, intended as "a satire, a prophecy or a blueprint" is still unclear.[5] What is clear is that just weeks before its publication, in an interview with the BBC, Huxley endorsed eugenicist measures designed to prevent the "rapid deterioration . . . of the whole West European stock."[6] The Nazis' own program of eugenics put paid to early enthusiasm for such ideas in the UK, but it is worth noting that well before that time notions of state control of reproduction had a significant popular appeal.[7]

But it is C. S. Lewis, alone among theologians, who offers us the most insightful understanding of the kind of world envisaged by genetic engineers. Originally provoked by a conversation with a scientific colleague at Oxford,[8] Lewis's fantasy *That Hideous Strength*, published in 1943, narrates a conversation between Lord Feverstone of NICE (the National Institute of Co-ordinated Experiments) and the young Mark Studdock, an ambitious Fellow of Bracton College:

The second problem [argues Feverstone] is our rivals on this planet. I don't mean only insects and bacteria. There's far too much life of every kind about, animal and vegetable. We haven't really cleared the place yet. First, we couldn't; and then we had aesthetic and humanitarian scruples; and we still haven't short-circuited the question of the balance of nature. All that is to be gone into. The third problem is Man himself.

Go on. This interests me very much.

Man has to take charge of Man. That means, remember, that some men have got to take charge of the rest—which is another reason for cashing in on it as soon as one can. You and I want to be the people who do the taking charge, not the ones who are taken charge of . . .

What sort of thing have you in mind?

Quite simple and obvious things, at first—sterilization of the unfit, liquidation of backward races (we don't want any dead weights), selective breeding. Then real education, including prenatal education. By real education I mean one that has no "take-it-or-leave-it" nonsense. A real education makes the patient what it wants infallibly: whatever he or his parents try to do about it. Of course, it'll have to be mainly psychological at first. But we'll get on to biochemical conditioning in the end and direct manipulation of the brain . . .

But this is stupendous, Feverstone.[9]

Baldly put, such designs appear not so much stupendous as fantastic, but the central point—as Lewis correctly grasps—is not about the details of the techniques as such (whether they be psychological, educational, biochemical, or genetic) but rather about power. As Lewis puts it, less prosaically, in his book *The Abolition of Man*, "For the power of man to make himself what he pleases means . . . the power of some men to make other men what *they* please."[10] Note how in Lewis's scenario the conquest of humanity is preceded by the conquest of animals and plants, indeed nature itself: ". . . what we call Man's power over Nature turns out to be a power exercised by some over other men with Nature as its instrument."[11]

We still have yet to learn from Lewis's prescience in this matter. Moralists and theologians go on supposing that an absolute dividing line can be drawn between the way we treat humans and nonhumans, utterly failing to see that for many scientists that dividing line has long since disappeared. The uncomfortable truth is that the now commonly accepted use of absolute power by humans over nonhumans in the matter of genetic manipulation is only the necessary experimental precursor to subsequent genetic manipulation of humanity itself.

Not incidentally, humans also share any adverse effects of the manipulation of animals. As early as 1857, social critic W. B. Adams sagely observed, "Our artificial breeding of animals produces in them many kinds of artificial disorders which recoil on their devourers."[12] The making of herbivores into carnivores by feeding them with offal from other animals, and the subsequent crisis about BSE, or "mad cow disease," is a classic example of where contempt for the natural lives of animals has rebounded on their manipulators.

In his farewell address, President Eisenhower said famously that we must be alert to the danger that "public policy could itself become the captive of the scientific technological elite." Christians and theologians eager not to appear defensive or reactionary, or both, have overwhelmingly failed to take on this scientific technological ascendancy. Elementary theological truths are now offered in public debate as though they were only "private, personal beliefs," of relevance solely to those who happen to hold them. The result is that the radical and necessary theological critique of genetic science as applied to animals and humans has gone largely by the board. Indeed, so unaware are churches generally about the issue that it may not surprise us to learn that the Church Commissioners in the UK until recently held substantial investments in the leading American corporation at the cutting edge of genetic engineering, and apparently without any moral qualms.[13]

But theology cannot be so easily shoved aside in the longer run, even despite the unadventurousness of its practitioners. This is because theological questions about "Who owns what?" "Who is responsible to whom?" and "What moral limits should we observe?" are all fundamentally human questions which sooner or later *have* to be confronted. Despite the apparently relentless, onward march of reproductive technologies, there remains a deep-seated public unease reflected in less than wholehearted endorsements for techniques such as transgenic animals and genetically modified foods. Surveying the evidence of discontent, one team of researchers concluded with this admirable understatement: "The prevailing focus of this ambivalence appears to be moral, a collection of anxieties about unforeseen dangers that may be involved in a range of technologies that are commonly perceived to be 'unnatural.'"[14]

Later on in 1946, Huxley said of *Brave New World* that if he were to rewrite it he would offer the Savage a "third alternative" in which "science and technology would be harnessed to serve rather than coerce humankind":

> Religion would be the conscious and intelligent pursuit of
> man's Final End, the unitive knowledge of the immanent
> Tao or Logos, the transcendent Godhead or Brahman.[15]

Interestingly enough, Lewis appeals to what he calls the doctrine of "the Tao," namely a notion of "natural law" found in all cultures and which includes respect for nature and natural objects.[16] The challenge and promise of this "third alternative" still awaits us.

13

Ethical Objections to Cloning

If cloning is here to stay, as some people seem to think, so is the accompanying controversy as well. Many people feel uneasy about cloning and what the practice might mean for human beings. Indeed, most discussion has almost entirely centered on the likely effects of the development of such techniques in relation to human subjects. In one sense, this is entirely understandable since, as we have seen, nonhuman "models" have often been just that: models for later work on human subjects.

But what such discussion misses is the need to address fundamental objections to the practice of cloning animals. Utilitarian justifications which have appeared in the press[1] tend to give the impression that ethical objections have been adequately dealt with. This is far from being the case. Anyone acquainted with the ethical literature about animal welfare and rights that has emerged over the last thirty years will have been struck by how even serious discussion in the media has been conducted in considerable ignorance of ethical work in this field.

In the light of this, it seems essential to highlight some of the basic issues that have not received anything like the consideration they deserve. In this chapter, I summarize five of these basic ethical and theological objections.

1. *Cloning represents an ethically regressive view of animals.* When we think of something as "progressive" we envisage that which is genuinely advancing, enlightening, improving, ameliorative, or bettering. In precisely these

senses there *has* been progress in our moral understanding of nonhuman animals. The change of perception can be described quite simply. It is a change
from the idea that animals are simply resources, commodities, machines, tools, here for our use or means
to human ends, to the realization that animals are sentient beings with their own intrinsic value, dignity, and
rights. This insight has been played out in a variety of
ways in a multitude of books, scholarly articles, and
papers[2] and, of course, various positions have been
taken. But the consensus of ethical and philosophical
opinion has shifted dramatically against an instrumentalist view of animals.

To give just one example: In a recent heavyweight
contribution, David DeGrazia offers a comprehensive
critique of current animal usage from a utilitarian perspective and concludes that "it is clear that the institution of factory farming, which causes massive harm
for trivial purposes, is ethically indefensible."[3] It is no
exaggeration to say that among those who have addressed the issue at length, the view that animals deserve our moral solicitude—that is, that they have a
right to have their interests taken into account and
that proper consideration of their interests should involve significant changes to our current lifestyle—is
uncontroversial.

In this context, the notion that animal cloning represents moral progress is obviously misplaced. Animals are not bettered, or improved, or ameliorated by
the act of cloning—indeed quite the reverse (see objection 2 following). What is most dominantly shown
in the act of cloning is that animals *can be* cloned—that
is, they are beings that can be manipulated, controlled, and exploited. To put no finer point on it: that
they are here for our use. But it is precisely this instrumentalist view of animals that has undergone such relentless ethical scrutiny and been found wanting.

It is sometimes argued that if it is right to farm and
kill animals for food then it must also be right to manipulate them genetically for research or farming. But
the two cases are logically and morally distinct. Even

if it can be shown that we may make use of animals in specific limited circumstances occasioned by genuine human need, it does not follow that we have the right to subordinate their life entirely to human needs or to take over their life as their absolute masters. Cloning represents a new tier of exploitation—the concretization of the old view that animals belong to us and are here for our use.

2. *Cloning renders animals liable to harm.* It is frequently overlooked that cloning experiments are just that: experiments. These experiments straddle the physiological adaptability of animals. It follows that while not all these experiments may cause actual, direct harm, some undoubtedly will do so. Published accounts of the first Edinburgh experiments in 1996 failed to report significant abnormalities. In addition to death through malformed internal organs, one lamb had to be delivered by caesarean section because it had grown to twice its normal size in the womb, and all but one of the five cloned lambs were at least 20 percent larger than they should have been.[4] Researcher Ian Wilmut is reported to have said that birth weights had been omitted because "no scientific meaning could be attached to them."[5] But whether they have scientific meaning or not, they clearly have moral significance and are relevant to any proper moral evaluation. We do not yet know all the details surrounding the latest cloning experiments, but the published report this time indicates significant abnormalities.[6] We shall be told, of course, that the harm suffered was minimal or nonexistent, and in some of these experiments that may have been the case. But what we can be reasonably certain of is that these experiments *risked* such harm and, in some cases at least, caused actual harm.

The infliction of such harm on animals is no light matter, and it is perplexing that recent discussion by the government and the media should have neglected this central issue. We should also be clear *why* it matters morally. Some people seek to justify the infliction of such harm on animals on the grounds that they are different from us. But are there any *morally relevant* differences between, say, a newborn child and a sentient animal? By common consent we find the infliction of harm and suffering upon children morally outrageous—and rightly so. But if we ask *why* that is so, the answer is, as we have seen, that they are vulnerable, defenseless, unprotected, morally innocent, and subjects of a special trust, and these considerations apply not only to newborn infants but also equally, if not more so, to animals.

Some utilitarians will resist this line and maintain that "benefit" can justify the infliction of either death or harm, or both. In this mode, we find the Science and Technology Committee of the U.K. parliament justifying cloning on the grounds of its "potential benefits." But on closer examination these "benefits" prove to be of a largely indirect, long-term, overstated kind. Indeed the difficulty in securing adequate justification is accepted by the Committee in this rather revealing line: "It is notoriously difficult to predict the benefits which will arise from a particular piece of research."[7] Quite so, but what is lost here is the ethical realization that such unpredictability and uncertainty count *against* the risking of actual harm to animals. Even in utilitarian terms the case has simply not been made. An appeal to some putative—and indirect—future benefit does not constitute a case of moral necessity. And what, in any case, is the supposedly compelling human need represented by such genetic manipulation? Nothing other than the creation of animals as bigger and better meat machines or laboratory tools.

3. *Cloning intensifies a morally reductionist view of animals.* Journalists who were invited to see "Dolly" in her pen and who photographed her profusely for the world's press were the willing participants in a massive public relations exercise. They perhaps can be forgiven for not reflecting on the invasive experimental procedures which caused her to be or, less obviously, on the previous experimental procedures that went so badly wrong. A healthy, appealing animal makes good copy. But a moment's reflection will surely lament the triumph of image over reality.

And that reality is the institutionalized, routine use of millions of animals today for research purposes. This involves the subjugation of animal life to human purposes in ways hitherto undreamt of in human history. This realization should give us some pause. Is it really self-evident that the nature of each and every species of life should be subordinated to human need and welfare, however indirect or hypothetical? There is an important distinction to be drawn between the individual human use of animals sometimes prompted by necessity and the institutionalization of such usage on a vast scale as it is today.[8] Moreover, even if *some* such use could be justified, it must be questioned whether now is the time to deploy yet another technique—in addition to all the other techniques of manipulation[9]—that will have the effect of more permanently reducing animals to designer products.

We stand at yet another moral crossroad in our relations with animals. Perhaps the best analogy is the emergence of industrialized—"factory"—farming in the 1960s. We were assured at the time that no animal would needlessly suffer, that intensive conditions would be in the animals' "best interests," and, most deceptively, that we could have *more*—and that more cheaply—without more cost to the animals. Thirty or so years later, we now know how fully deceived we were and that the costs—and not only to the animals concerned but also to ourselves—were considerably greater than had been supposed.[10] Moreover, only now are we beginning to dismantle some of the inhumane systems —the veal crate, the sow stall, the battery cage—that were previously lauded for their technical ingenuity. Perhaps it is not going too far to say that while in the 1960s we began to *treat* animals as machines, now in the 1990s we have begun to *make* them machines.

4. *Cloning involves the commercial degradation of animal life.* In a moment of rare candor, former Archbishop John Habgood wrote of the motives behind cloning experiments:

But should science be going down this road at all? What is the point of it? The simple answer is—money. The driving force behind most of the research in this field has come from the agricultural industry. I use the word industry deliberately. Cloning is a means of standardizing products, and that is what industry always wants.[11]

The statement is all the more remarkable because Habgood, while cautious, is not opposed to animal cloning. The gist of his article is that what we do to animals should not justify what may be done to human beings. His argument deserves some scrutiny: "Even those who do not believe in God generally recognize a quality of 'otherness' in people," he maintains. "People are not things to be controlled or manipulated; they are other beings, with their own consciousness of being, to whom we relate and respond."[12] The puzzle here is how all human subjects could be included within such a definition, and thereby protected against cloning, but not nonhuman subjects as well. To deny that we can detect "otherness" in animals, and that animals too are self-conscious, is to fly in the face of substantial scientific evidence.[13]

But note the underlying argument: Animals can be controlled and manipulated purely for money and convenience—just because they are animals. This putative total dividing line morally between how we treat animals and how we treat humans really will not stand up. Indeed Habgood's own commendable caution leads him to conclude tentatively in this direction. To assimilate living beings into "a mechanical model" might "on a superficial view promise greater freedom and prosperity." "On the contrary," he concludes, "the more we treat animal life as being manipulable for human convenience, the greater the temptation to think of human life in similar terms."[14] Indeed so. But it is so precisely because the absolute distinction (in terms of moral treatment) between humans and nonhumans previously supposed is insupportable. What we do to animals—as sentient, self-conscious, intelligent be-ings—does influence our understanding of moral lim-its, or lack of them, in relation to other sentient, self-conscious, intelligent . . . human subjects. The stark moral truth must be unmasked: Not satisfied with simply exploiting animals, we now presume to change their nature in order to do so more profitably. In the chilling words of one research scientist, ". . . we can design the whole carcass, if you like, from embryo to plate to meet a particular market niche."[15]

5. *Cloning represents a spiritually impoverished view of animals.* Perhaps the most disturbing aspect of recent discus-sion has been the attempt to relegate to the sidelines, or even silence altogether, theological objections to cloning.[16] This is disturbing because while sometimes presented as considerations only relevant to the nar-row confines of religious believers, they often raise wider issues that desperately need a hearing in order to gain some perspective on scientific developments. Let me give three examples.

First, while proponents of cloning often appeal in a straightforwardly utilitarian way to "benefit," their un-derstanding of what benefits the human species is of-ten remarkably narrow. What informs the Science and Technology Committee's defense of cloning is *inter alia* a sense of "scientific vistas," the likely profits of the pharmaceutical industry and, of course, an appeal to medical spin-offs.[17] These considerations are more or less worthy ones, but they are not the only ones. What is not addressed, for example, is the debit side in-volved in developing techniques that treat animals as machines, or the likely social and institutional effects of so doing. Are humans really benefited by a wholly utilitarian and instrumentalist understanding of other sentient creatures? At least it is a question worth ad-dressing.

Second, the Science and Technology Committee rightly points out that the regulatory framework gov-erning animal experiments applies to the Edinburgh cloning experiments. The regulatory system is in-tended to ensure that no "unnecessary suffering" is caused to animals.[18] But beyond this bland assurance is the seldom addressed issue of moral limits. That issue is persistently sidestepped by reference to the regulatory system, whereas anyone with any knowledge of regulatory systems knows that they invariably *manage* rather than *address* ethical questions. Hence the illusion is created that the issue of moral limits has been adequately faced when in fact it actually has been bypassed.

The issue is this: Is it right to manipulate animals genetically—that is, to change their God-given nature—in order to increase profitability and convenience? That issue was pinpointed in a recent address on industrialized farming by an unlikely advocate of animal rights, the Prince of Wales. On genetic manipulation, he questioned, "What actual right do we have to experiment, Frankenstein-like, with the very stuff of life?" He continued:

> We live in an age of rights. It seems to me that it is about time our Creator had rights too. I believe we have now reached a moral and ethical watershed beyond which we venture into realms that belong to God, and to God alone.[19]

Some will find this line unconvincing or alarmist, or both, but it contains the germ of an important theological truth. I have expressed it elsewhere by arguing that animals have rights because God their Creator has the right to see that creation is treated with respect.[20] This insight is not just available to those who believe in God or the rights of God's creatures. The essential point is that there are moral limits to what humans may do to change the intrinsic nature and integrity of other sentient beings—even in pursuit of apparently worthy ends.

Third, reference has already been made to the notion of the "intrinsic value" of animals. Such an idea does not explicitly require a theistic view of the world, but it is clearly consonant with it, and obviously makes sense within it. For if God is the loving Creator of all, everything created—especially beings with sentience and intelligence—has value in itself because God made it. From this standpoint, the value of other living beings is tied up with the confession of a Creator God who guarantees the objective value of what is created. All this is not to deny that theists generally, and Christians in particular, have historically anything other than a poor record on animal protection but, equally, we should not overlook how the same tradition can provide a positive, theologically grounded, defense of animals.

Failure to grasp these points has meant that commentators—even, and especially, Christian ones—frequently lapse into a kind of moral parochialism when it comes to discussions about animals, as if God only cared for one of the millions of species in the created world. This, in turn, has led to a practical form of idolatry. By "idolatry" I mean here the deification of the human species by regarding human beings as the sole, main, or even exclusive concern of God the Creator.[21] The treatment of animals often appears a small issue to Christians, but if the doctrine of God the Creator is taken seriously, it means, at the very least, that an estimate of our own needs and welfare is not the only basis on which we should judge our relations with the animal world.

14

Bishops Say No to Fur

In previous chapters I have been very critical of the churches and their failures to take animal rights seriously. It gives me special joy therefore to be able to narrate one courageous and prophetic stand by bishops against cruelty.

The fur industry gobbles up tens of millions of wild animals every year, either trapped in the wild or killed in fur factories. Just one example will suffice: One of the most common traps used is the steel-jawed leghold trap in which the animal is caught for hours, days, even weeks, during which it suffers thirst, exhaustion, and hunger—not to mention the gnawing pain produced by the jaws of the trap itself. While banned in the United Kingdom for more than forty years, it remains one of the most commonly used methods of trapping the millions of wild animals in the United States and Canada.

Until recently the only Christian voices heard on this matter had been *in defense* of fur trapping. In 1986 the Anglican and Roman Catholic bishops of Northern Canada issued a statement expressing their "solidarity" with those "who are engaged in a struggle to save fur trapping as a way of life."[1] Not one word of their defense expressed any concern for the suffering that the animals had to undergo. Astonished at their statement and appalled lest their verdict be taken as the only Christian view of the matter, I encouraged the antifur organization, Lynx, to approach U.K. bishops, inviting them to endorse a contrary statement that they would not buy or wear fur.

An impressive number of Anglican bishops, forty-one in all, responded favorably. The list included twelve diocesan bishops; the former Archbishop of Canterbury, Donald Coggan; and the Primus of the Scottish Episcopal Church, Richard Holloway. I edited the book *Cruelty and Christian Conscience*, which listed the names of the bishops who had signed the pledge, together with fifteen individual episcopal statements.[2] The Archbishop of Wales wrote a foreword to the book, welcoming the statements by his episcopal colleagues that "fur-bearing animals inextricably belong to God's created order." The book also contained a lengthy theological introduction and a factual chapter highlighting the precise cruelties involved in fur production.

Bearing in mind the power of the international multimillion-dollar fur industry, the book was a triumph for Christian conscience over commercial gain. Moreover it showed quite graphically that the easy endorsement of trapping practices by the Canadian bishops was not going to go unchallenged. It constituted the most united Christian front against cruelty this century. As one not entirely friendly journalist remarked to me, "I'm amazed that over forty Anglican bishops can agree about anything."

Bishops are not infrequently accused of failing to speak out against animal cruelty, but what happens when they do? The response to this publication will go down in the annals of animal rights history. The first response was no response. The "quality" U.K. papers, including *The Times* and the *Guardian*, ignored it. Only the *Daily Telegraph* covered the story by finding one beleaguered bishop who had a fur-lined robe and who was reluctant to bury it. Par for the course, one might say. But it was the coverage in the church press that was the most revealing. Excepting the fair coverage in the *Church of England Newspaper*[3], the *Church Times* squeezed in a dismissive paragraph.

Two weeks later, Bishop Hugh Montefiore used his column in the same newspaper to launch a bitter attack on the bishops for their actions, arguing that they had not enhanced "the reputation of their episcopal offices."[4] The lines of attack were specious to say the least. One "senior diocesan bishop" was criticized for stating that "Fur-bearing animals living in the wild are not humanely killed" and that such "generalizations are dangerous when detailed investigation is omitted"—completely ignoring the ten pages of factual evidence in the book.

More extraordinary still, the same senior bishop was taken to task for the "generalization" that "Fur is not nowadays necessary for human survival as it was in the cold climates of the distant past." All that Montefiore could muster by way of refutation, however, consisted of personal anecdotal evidence (a visit to Russia) and a request from his daughter living over there for furs for herself and her friends.

Most tendentious of all was Montefiore's claim that it is difficult "in principle" to draw a distinction between fur farming and other forms of husbandry. As the book indicated, however, special factors pertain to fur farming which do not necessarily apply to other forms of farming, the chief one being the level of stress and suffering caused when wild animals are restricted to small, barren cages. This is the view of competent bodies, for example the U.K. government's own Farm Animal Welfare Council. His attack was even more extraordinary since Montefiore was a member (as was I) of a Working Party which specifically and unanimously recommended minimum "basic guidelines" for animal husbandry which do not "deny the environmental requirements of the basic behavioral needs of the animals"[5]— guidelines which clearly preclude fur farming. In the light of Montefiore's subsequent defense of hunting on the grounds that we have a "prior duty" to farmed animals, his position is shown to be inconsistent at best.[6]

Then came, predictably enough, the onslaught from Canada. The Canadian bishops had got wind of the U.K. bishops' statement and launched a fierce counterattack. The *Church Times* allowed the Canadian bishops two subsequent blasts on page two and sided with them in an editorial. "The dispute illustrates," opined the editor, John Whale, "how difficult it is to make ethical rules of practice which have universal application"—a view which might have come close to carrying conviction if that newspaper's coverage hadn't actually obscured the ethical issue itself.[7]

But what were the arguments precisely? The anti-fur campaign, according to the nine Canadian bishops of the North, including the Canadian primate, "violates the dignity of the aboriginal peoples and their traditions." Indeed the Bishop of the Arctic in a letter to the forty-one UK bishops went further: Not only had such campaigns "destroyed (sic) the Inuit and Indian people of my diocese economically, they are destroying them spiritually and emotionally."[8] Indeed, a subsequent BBC television program, "Everyman," devoted more than sixty minutes to a highly positive profile of the Bishop of the Arctic, in which the book was singled out for attack and not one counter-balancing view of the fur trade was allowed air time.

All this may appear deeply humane and compassionate. Who could be against the rights of indigenous peoples? The implication is obvious: Those who care for animals care little for humans. The arguments for animal welfare are exposed for what they truly are: anti-people, pure and simple. As Oscar Wilde remarked, however, "The truth is seldom pure and rarely simple."

Carol McKenna of Respect for Animals has shown how in the two territories of Canada where most indigenous people live—the Yukon and the Northwest Territories—44,690 animals were trapped in one season alone. Hence of the fifty million wild animals which are killed each year, the "fur from native peoples represents *less than one tenth of one per cent of the world's fur trade.*"[9] And if we ask how it is that the rights of indigenous people figure so prominently in a debate to which they are almost completely irrelevant, the answer is almost as cynical. In order to combat the increasing unpopularity of fur, the industry and the Canadian government were advised as early as 1985 to utilize "contradictory emotional themes of interest to the same target publics, e.g. preservation of traditional indigenous cultures."[10] As one New Brunswick "fur-bearer biologist" admitted frankly, "The reason you hear the native side so much is that it is the most effective argument to keep us *all* trapping."[11]

In short, indigenous peoples were used as a public relations ploy to maintain the fur industry against the success of the anti-fur campaign. The plight of indigenous people so heralded by Canadian bishops has much more to do with saving national exports than preserving indigenous culture. The Canadian government helped finance the visit of one native chief who appeared on the doorstep of the then Bishop of London—one of the signatories of the anti-fur book.[12] The words of one press release issued by the Canadian government cannot be denied: "The fur industry contributes an estimated $600 million annually to the Canadian economy," and also revealingly, "Over 80 per cent of Canadian wild fur production is exported—three-quarters of which is destined for the European market."[13]

All in all then, the U.K. bishops have every right to feel that their principled stand received pretty shoddy treatment—not least of all at the hands of the church press; the argument of the book even when allowed to be heard was misrepresented and overlaid with otiose arguments at best. The thesis of the book was not concerned about the subsistence use of animals but about cruelty for fashion fur. The question of the supposed "necessity" for fur was raised and answered explicitly in the book itself.

To show that something is morally necessary we have to show that it is essential, unavoidable, or, arguably, that some higher good requires it which could not in any way be obtained without it. Can fur trapping and/or ranching be classified in these terms? It is not impossible to conceive of some situations in which warm clothing in cold climates was essential for human survival. Whether this conceivable situation ever was an actual situation may be a subject of some dispute. For myself, I am prepared to accept that it may well have been essential for human survival in some circumstances, somewhere and at some point. But even if we accept that this was once the case, it still has to be shown that fur wearing is essential today.

Now some church people have argued that fur trapping is morally justifiable because it is "a way of life deeply rooted in the cultural traditions of the aboriginal societies in the Canadian North." Even if this is true—and not all would accept that it is or has always been true—it does not settle the question of strict moral necessity. Cultural traditions may well be admirable things and on the whole we look favorably upon them. But not *all* practices within a culture can be claimed as morally necessary simply because we sometimes judge that human culture is generally of value. Indeed, there is, morally speaking, only a very limited argument that can be made from cultural traditions.

Some cultures may contain practices (such as infanticide, or female circumcision, or human sacrifice) which are immoral or evil, and some cultures based on such practices may well be immoral or evil as a whole. Even if we suppose that once upon a time some trapping of animals for clothing in some cultures was morally essential for human survival, that still does not answer the issue that such practices must nowadays be shown to be essential in order to qualify as justifiable.

It is here, of course, that we reach the rub. For whatever may have been true in the past, it is now impossible to claim that the wearing of furs is essential to human survival. We need to remind ourselves that fashion and adornment or the enjoyment of luxury do not constitute anything approximating moral necessity. Without such necessity the case for furs collapses.[14]

Other critics made much of the fact that the statement signed by the bishops pledged not to buy or wear fur. Some indeed lampooned the notion that individual actions of this kind were anything other than vestiges of puritanism and ethically naive. But, again, these objections were both anticipated and addressed in the book and put in their proper context:

> We anticipate three objections. In the first place, it is sometimes suggested that individual acts of renunciation—such as refusing to buy or wear certain products— are ludicrously individualistic gestures inappropriate to the formidable multinational systems of trade and business with which we nowadays have to contend. But what this objection overlooks is that almost all these systems depend upon individual customers being prepared to buy their products or, at least, not thinking very carefully about how such products are acquired. Movements against cruelty have to begin somewhere, and there are good reasons why Christians at least should begin with themselves—examining their own roles as shoppers and consumers. The international trade in furs will die when people no longer want to buy them.
>
> The second objection argues that the British are terribly good at condemning cruelty perpetuated overseas whilst turning a blind eye to cruelty nearer home. The fact is, however, that while fur trapping takes place overseas,

fur farming takes place in many European countries—not least of all in the United Kingdom. British people wear fur reared and killed on British farms. Even if we restrict ourselves to that issue alone, the abuse of animals on British soil calls for some exercise of national responsibility. But in reality animal protection knows no national boundaries. Precisely because cruelty is organized on a multinational basis, it requires an international response.

The third objection is that it is partial and selective to choose *this* one issue of animal cruelty when there are so many other areas of animal abuse and exploitation. It is certainly true that animal cruelty is still widespread and I, for one, think that there needs to be a much wider—internationally coordinated—campaign against cruelty in all its forms. Nevertheless, we need to repeat that movements against cruelty must begin *somewhere* and that somewhere should be where individuals can make a difference. If there is to be progressive disengagement from cruelty to animals, it has to start where people can effectively make choices. Perhaps it is not irrelevant to recall here the long ascetical tradition within Christianity which has always invited individual believers to scrutinize their way of life and to give up even pleasurable things if they stand in the way of achieving some spiritual good. What is at stake in the way we use and abuse animals is our own spiritual understanding—or lack of it—of our own place in creation. Manifold abuse of animals should not obscure for us the real choices we are able to make which affect the lives and suffering of millions of sentient creatures.[15]

15

Works of Darkness, Signs of Light

Some people may be uneasy with my metaphor of light and dark. It might appear to suggest a wholly black-and-white approach to the complexity of our exploitation of animals. But, in my view, there is something dark—in the proper sense of that word, namely "unenlightened"—about much of what we do to animals. That is why I write of our maltreatment of animals as stemming from a kind of spiritual blindness—a failure to see animals for what they are: God's creatures with their own intrinsic worth and value.

One personal recollection may help. When I was in my young teens, despite my sympathy for animals, I used to go fishing. In the heavily working-class culture into which I was born there was nothing exceptional about that. I was never encouraged to look upon fish as beings that could feel, or to think that the act of hooking fish might actually cause them pain. It was only when I had to disgorge a hook from a poor creature's stomach—and saw it reeling in my hands—that I began to have real doubts.

I recount this experience not in a spirit of "unholier than thou" but only to underline the fact that we are all, at one level or another, agents of darkness, that is, of unenlightened thoughts and actions toward animals. Far from wanting to "demonize" opponents, I want all of us, animal advocates included, to appreciate the struggle between light and darkness that goes on within the souls of all of us.[1]

Over the years, I have received thousands of letters from activists, many of which have been deeply sustaining and for which

I am immensely grateful. But there have always been some that have disturbed me, and one especially. It was a letter from an American animal advocate who wrote that while some people idolized film stars, she idolized the leaders of the animal-rights movement and, to my horror, she included me among them. Don't misunderstand me: It is great to be thought well of and I know what this person meant when she spoke of how some people are especially gifted in being able to inspire others. I have had many heroes in my life and my deepest wish is that my contribution has been to help inspire people to take the whole animal issue more seriously. But wanting to be an inspiration is one thing; being idolized is another. I had to write back—utterly without understatement—that I was only a sinner like her—only more so.

The very most that can be said of any of us is that we are, in Nehru's words, "little men [or women] who support a great cause." Idolizing or demonizing either our champions or our opponents betrays a fundamental failure to understand the biblical doctrine of common sinfulness, specifically our broken and estranged humanity. I now never speak, as I confess I once did, of particular people as "leaders" of the movement. I now see that this is to burden us—and especially them—with too much expectation and to invite inevitable disappointment.

Over the years too, I have heard many confessions, not least of all from people who exploit animals. People have said how they notionally appreciate the animal issue but still love hunting, bullfighting, coursing, shooting. These people were not being disingenuous; they knew there was something wrong in enjoying these things but they couldn't help themselves. I do not believe that these were evil people, and I abhor personal attacks on individuals who are after all, like the rest of us, combinations of light and dark. But, on the other hand, I do think that such exploitation is objectively evil and, often without knowing it, we are all to some extent involved, directly or indirectly, in evil actions. Whatever its limitations as a statement of moral theology, the judgment of the papal encyclical *Veritatis Splendor* is basically sound and worth repeating: There are intrinsically evil acts, that is disordered acts "incapable of being ordered to God and the good of the human person."[2]

But an animal rights position based on describing certain acts as evil, however important that realization may be in itself, is insufficient as a strategy for change. We need to understand *why* people do these things to animals. Negative labeling of individuals betokens an insufficiently sophisticated understanding of the nature of evil itself.

In any case the massive exploitation of animals in the world today is not, in the main, the result of many thousands or millions of people *deciding* to abuse animals. Indeed, very few people decide—in the sense of rationally weighing up the pros and cons—anything at all. The decisions have almost entirely been made for them. People do not choose to kill for food; they find meat packaged for them in the supermarket. People do not choose to inflict suffering on animals in laboratories; they simply utilize pharmaceutical products prescribed for them. People do not choose to put hens in batteries; they simply buy the cheapest eggs; and so on. We are all caught in deeply ingrained habits of life that constrain our field of moral action and awareness.

Given that modern society is so inextricably based on animal exploitation—so much so that even vegans cannot claim to be pure—many people simply despair of the possibility of fundamental moral change. Whether we like it or not, we are all involved in cycles of exploitation and violence toward animals, and we are all thus compromised. Indeed one commentator, usually sympathetic to animal concerns, surveyed the current exploitation of humans and exclaimed that "to talk of animal rights in this context is absurd"—as if, illogically, the exploitation of one species meant that one had to be blind to the exploitation of others.

Nevertheless, for all its illogicality, this view does represent a current fatalism about animal abuse. The best we can do, it is supposed, is to save some humans from injustice: As for animals, the sporadic suppression of the grossest kind of cruelty is probably the best we can manage. What fuels this kind of fatalism is a failure to see how the world can be changed. People often cannot imagine a world without animal exploitation, especially without multimillion-dollar capitalist industries which deal in animal products. Before such powerful, almost supra-human, agencies, individual moral sensibility appears like a flower waiting to be crushed by a juggernaut.

But it is precisely here, where all seems dark, or at least at its darkest, that I believe there is the possibility of light. Can we change from institutionalized systems of exploitation to nonexploitative ones? Can the great multinationals that gobble up millions of animals every year really be turned around? I think the answer is yes, and—with God's help—it can and will be done.

"But *how* precisely?" some will ask. As a former vice president of the United States once said, "Predictions are hazardous because they concern the future." Allowing for that truism, I sketch six evolutionary, yet overlapping, processes of transformation that offer hope for the future.

The first stage begins with individual spiritual realization. Here animal advocates do not begin with a blank page. A great many people do not like killing animals and many recoil from the deliberate infliction of suffering. This "instinctive" (for want of a better word) sympathy for animals is found in all societies and cultures. It is amply documented in works of poetry and literature. However, it is often derided as "childish." "Grown-ups" grow up, it seems, by discarding these childish feelings for animals. A good example is provided by Seamus Heaney in his poem "The Early Purges." He describes his not unnatural horror as a child at witnessing kittens being drowned, but later reflects as an adult that "living displaces false sentiments."[3] It is sad to see a poet of such insight falling for a version of emotional political correctness. In fact, these "childlike" senses of kinship with animals are packed with spiritual significance and testify at the deepest level to the work of divine grace within us.

To be personal for a moment: I have seen firsthand the operation of such grace in the lives of my four children. All of them are committed vegetarians. Some may cynically conclude that such is the result of fatherly indoctrination, but they would be mistaken. None of them have been forced to be vegetarian, and the option of eating "dead animals" (as my son correctly describes meat) is always open to them. No, what we have done rather as parents is to liberate the vegetarian in them: the desire in almost all children not to kill living things. It is this deep-seated desire to live without killing which is usually quashed by meat-eating parents. Currently many millions of veggie-to-be children have no choice but to live with their carnivorous parents who do all they can to prevent their own offspring from being "abnormal," which more often than not includes the enforcement of a meat-based diet.

This then is the first stage: recognizing and finding space for an ethical appreciation of living creatures. I begin with food because this is the point at which most humans have contact with animals and is easily the most corrosive of moral sense, especially at an early stage. Simply being a vegetarian in the context of a carnivorous society demonstrates an ethical alternative. Carnivorous grown-ups are often very defensive about vegetarian children or vegetarian adults, and for this reason especially: We are a living challenge to the easygoing acceptance of the necessity of killing for food.

What currently spurs on the animal-rights movement in the United Kingdom and the United States more than anything else is this: the realization that it isn't necessary to eat meat. Young animal-sensitive people are now taking revenge on their carnivorous parents. The growth of vegetarianism among the fourteen-to-eighteen age group has been startling. According to my calculations, based on the Social Attitudes Survey in the United Kingdom, there are now more vegetarians, demi-vegetarians, and vegans than practicing Roman Catholics in this country.[4]

What was once judged "childish sentimentality," a natural but essentially retarded moral disposition, has become established as an ethical option. Once derided as a matter of "taste," it is now rightly seen as a question of justice. The first and essential task of the animal-rights movement then is to champion and liberate the innate human sensibility for other creatures.

The second process is to help people relate their ethical sensibility to contemporary practice. In one way animal advocates have been the victims of their own success. One of the first concerns of the RSPCA, as the first national anti-cruelty organization in the world, was not only to make slaughter more "humane" but also to outlaw the public slaughter of farm animals.[5] Doubtless there were good reasons why this should be done, not least of all because of the brutalizing effect of such public spectacles. But this welcome reform has had one unfortunate result: It removed slaughter from public gaze so that the direct relationship between the act of slaughter and the act of eating meat became obscure. In short, the slaughter of animals has become all but publicly invisible.

The result has been that only a few who have visited private or public slaughterhouses have seen for themselves the barbarity involved in killing. It is really quite astonishing to meet intelligent and conscientious people who really have no idea of how their meat comes to their plate or of the fallible and frequently cruel methods of contemporary slaughter. Here is just one example: Very few appreciate that thirty million or more male chicks—the unwanted counterparts to hens in battery cages—in the United Kingdom are gassed, suffocated, or homogenized (fed through chopping machines *en masse*) within seventy-two hours of birth.

The contemporary invisibility of animal abuse, whether in farming or research, bolsters up a spurious public confidence that is only shaken when the media, especially television, show people what is really going on. Even now television companies are highly reticent about showing "real footage" of animal abuse, and what does go out in news broadcasts is heavily edited for viewing sensibility. Understandable as such reserve may be, the undeniable result is to distance individuals from cognizance of the reality of slaughter and cruelty. The task then of animal societies is to make the invisible visible, to unmask and uncover the true picture so that people can see for themselves. There is a direct and fundamental correlation between sight and sensibility: What we do not see, we cannot meaningfully appropriate for ourselves.

In this area, there is much to be done and much that has already been done. Chief among the successes has been the work of undercover investigators who have provided documentary evidence of what happens in transport, laboratories, markets, and slaughterhouses, often at great risk to themselves. Two recent reports, one on conditions in the world's zoos by the Born Free Foundation and the World Society for the Protection of Animals, and the other on the treatment of animals in British markets by

Animal Aid, are exemplary in their thoroughness.[6] Anyone who doubts the savagery toward animals in contemporary society need only view the range of documentary films and videos available from the major animal societies.[7]

It may seem overconfident to suppose that when confronted with the reality of killing and cruelty people will register a moral problem, or even make the necessary moral adjustment to their lifestyle. Surely, it may be protested, some people are utterly desensitized, as some have undoubtedly become to television pictures of, for example, children starving. Well, some may be, perhaps some will always be so desensitized. But equally some, perhaps (as I think) the majority, will not be. And here is the continuing window of opportunity for animal advocates. Visual contact, doubtless, is not itself enough, but it is one factor among many that can help spur on full ethical realization.

The third process is to place ethical concern for animals on the intellectual agenda. Feeling for animals and seeing firsthand the realities of animal exploitation must go hand in hand with an appreciation that ethical sensitivity has a strong rational basis. The debate about animal rights is not about aesthetic taste but about moral truth. Over many years, animal societies have pioneered the inclusion of humane education in the classroom, and organizations such as the RSPCA and International Fund for Animal Welfare (IFAW) now offer first-rate educational material.[8] But in addition to this important work, animal societies need to engage a wider intellectual debate. Slowly but surely normative ethical questions about our treatment of animals are beginning to make their mark on courses in ethics, theology, and philosophy, backed by an impressive array of course material.[9] This intellectual debate is an essential prerequisite to social and moral change. Animal societies must move from seeking to program the truth to ensuring that truth is on the program.

As already noted, most of the intellectual work on animals over the last twenty years has been progressive in orientation. Animal exploitation thrives both on secrecy and intellectual neglect. What is needed over the years ahead are college and university courses where there can be rigorous intellectual debate about the status of animals. Animal societies need to ensure the full institutionalization of this debate by funding—without any strings—courses, lectures, journals, academic posts, indeed academies themselves, that will further serious ethical inquiry. There needs to be investment in the intellectual debate about animals at a new and higher level of education.

The obvious parallel here is with the development of feminism. Twenty or so years ago people would have laughed (indeed did laugh) at the idea of courses in women's studies. Now such courses, posts, even departments, are established in colleges and universities all over the world. The assumptions of patriarchy are now regularly subjected to academic scrutiny and debate. Now is the time for animal advocates to invest in the power of their ideas and also in a no less rigorous scrutiny of the opposing ideology, namely speciesism. Not least of all is the need for theological institutions, seminaries, theological colleges, and university departments of theology to begin to offer specifically theological courses of study which encompass questions relating to the nonhuman creation.

I can give some personal testimony here. When my post at Oxford was announced in 1992 there were some people, even animal advocates, who were unsure that animal welfare resources should be spent on academic teaching and research. Money for animal welfare should be spent directly on animal welfare, it was claimed. But over the years, partly as a result of my own work and that of others, there has been an increasing appreciation that there can be no long-term future for animal protection without challenging many of the pivotal ideas that justify animal abuse. It is not enough that people should be kind to animals (though that itself, of course, is a welcome advance); it is also vitally important that people understand why animals deserve our solicitude and our respect. We shall not change the world for animals without also changing people's ideas about the world.

In fact, my post at Oxford—and the other similar posts concerned with ethics that have now been created around the world—are part of a wider feature of the animal-rights movement that has emerged over recent years. It is the willingness to do intellectual battle so that the claims of animals are heard and their case presented at every level of society. People who want to use animals, whether it be in university departments of zoology, or for wildlife films (where the use of animals is frequently far from benign) or even for routine school dissection—to take only three examples—now have to face the intellectual challenge as never before. In short, they have to confront new questions, to think again, and to justify their actions. One of the most gratifying remarks I hear from students or colleagues after lecturing—and I believe that it is in most cases sincerely said—is that they have been forced to rethink their position. Thinking and arguing are not all there is to moral change but, no less than feeling or experience, they can provide one valuable stimulus to reevaluation.

The fourth process is to institutionalize informed ethical choice. The truth is that in modern capitalist society we have great power as consumers, shoppers, taxpayers, and investors. As already noted, until now those who want to choose ethically have had virtually no choice. But cracks are beginning to appear in what previously was something like a wall of resistance to change.

Thanks to a variety of pioneers, we now have some measure of ethical choice in some unexpected quarters. Lady Dowding's establishment of the international Beauty Without Cruelty organization, derided at the time of its inception as hopelessly visionary, has laid the ground for successive far-reaching developments, notably Anita Roddick's founding of The Body Shop and her implacable opposition to animal testing for cosmetics.[10] Now, for the first time, people can see in the high street highly competitive (some would add superior) alternatives to the usual range of toiletries tested on animals. No less remarkable is the well-publicized policy of the Co-operative Bank which refrains from investing in companies which test cosmetics on animals.[11] In the field of investment generally, there are now a range of societies which offer "ethical investment" exclusive of the normal agencies of animal abuse. Added to this has been the welcome development by the RSPCA in establishing "Freedom Foods," that is, meat products where the care of animals has had to meet certain minimum standards.[12]

Of course none of these developments are without their own problems—not least of all of consistency. For example, since almost all ingredients for cosmetics have been tested at one time or another in their history on animals, there is no absolutely pure land possible, and even The Body Shop has had to accept some kind of artificial cutoff point (usually five years since they were originally tested). Again the criteria for the RSPCA's "Freedom Foods" do not currently disavow non-veterinary mutilations such as the tail docking of pigs or debeaking in the case of hens—procedures which indubitably cause suffering.[13] Nevertheless, while one can legitimately quarrel with some aspects of these developments, they are at least in the right direction and deserve our warm support.

But mechanisms for ethical choice are always bound to be problematic unless "informed" choice is facilitated as well. It is not enough that people can choose; it is vital that they are given the information *that enables them* to choose. Hence the question of accurate labeling is vital. Sometimes people deride the notion of commercially viable ethical choice by citing as an example the failure of most people to buy free range eggs. "No use blaming the farmer," they say, "since most consumers will only buy cheap, battery produced eggs." But what is often overlooked is that the sales of free range eggs have to compete commercially on uneven terms. While at last many free range eggs are so labeled, it is not so with battery eggs.

To those who say "consumers will always buy the cheapest whatever the cost to the animals," we should reply, "let the consumers be given accurate information about where their food comes from and how it was produced." For this to happen it is vital that all battery eggs are clearly labeled as "eggs from hens in cages," and similarly appropriate information should appear on all meat or animal-derived products. Now is the time to put the rhetoric about consumer choice to the test: By all means let people decide but on the basis of accurate labeling of these products. We know how much this is resisted by animal exploiters. Alan Clark, former minister in a previous British Conservative administration, recalls his long fight to get accurate labeling of fur products, and how his attempts were finally defeated by political pressure exercised by the then Prime Minister, Margaret Thatcher, troubled by the possible repercussions on her impending visit to Canada.[14]

The fifth process of change concerns legislative advance for animals. During the last five years there has been an attempt by some animal rightists to distance themselves from animal welfare and to insist on "abolitionist only" legislation with regard to animals. I think it is a great mistake to place animal rights and animal welfare in juxtaposition, as if they were two wholly incompatible philosophies. An even worse mistake, in my view, is to suppose that an animal rights position is *opposed* to that of animal welfare. Of course, some conceptions of animal welfare are remarkably weak, and we now have the phenomenon of animal exploiters, especially hunters and researchers, paying lip service to the notion in theory while actually disregarding what it means in practice. But however much the concept may be misused, animal advocates should not abandon it; there is no essential contradiction between caring for an animal's well-being and respect for its rights.

There are of course important differences concerning matters of principle and pragmatic orientation within the community of animal advocates, and they require sober, thoughtful discussion. That there are differences among what is an increasingly large and multifaceted movement for social change is to be expected. But it is a great folly to suppose that there is only *one* strategy for change (save of course for my caveat about violence and illegality) or indeed only one blueprint for legislative advance that all animal advocates must adopt. Historically all legislative change on any vexed moral issue—from slavery to capital punishment—has been a gradualist, piecemeal affair.

I have already made clear my view that animal advocates should embrace gradualism and work consistently and pragmatically (and professionally) for change, and this is especially true of legislative advance. There is no contradiction between holding long-term goals and working pragmatically for their progressive realization. Indeed, there is an obligation to do so. From the standpoint of the animals we seek to represent, we should do all we can to benefit their position and alleviate their suffering.

For example, I wholly agree with the approach of most people in the Labor Party in the United Kingdom in moving against hunting with hounds but not, in the present climate, against angling.

For myself, I'm against causing pain to any living creature for sport, and that most definitely includes angling. On the other hand, there are two good reasons for supporting Labor's current position. The first is theoretical and the second is pragmatic. While fish undoubtedly experience pain, the case that *all* fish suffer (bearing in mind that there is an important distinction between pain and suffering) is less strong than in the case of mammals. Second, while I would certainly support legislation to ban fishing, it makes good pragmatic sense to push hardest at those practices which enjoy little public support and also, crucially, where there is the political will for change.

To those who argue that this is morally inconsistent, the answer has to be that in a democratic society all legislative advance for animals has to work from a basis of popular support. This always involves some kind of inconsistency in practice since public opinion is itself frequently inconsistent. But from the standpoint of animal protection there is really no alternative: To fail to support one proposal because it is inconsistent in not embracing another is a recipe for perpetual inaction. If this standpoint had been adopted in the nineteenth century, the most rudimentary anticruelty legislation such as now exists in the United Kingdom would not have been enacted.

It is, however, important that legislation should be genuinely progressive, that is, moving toward the longer-term goal and not actually hindering it. It is therefore obviously not sensible or pragmatic to support legislation which helps some animals only *at the expense* of others. Neither is it prudent to adopt legislation which bolsters up existing unethical practice. In this latter category I include the recent attempt to adopt "humane trapping standards" which—to put it crudely—are nothing less than a confidence trick. Trapping wild animals through leg-hold traps is inherently cruel. There is—through leg traps at least—no uncruel way of trapping such animals. "Humane standards" create an illusion of non-cruelty and are earnestly advanced by the fur-trapping industry for that reason.

There are, however, some legislative advances which fall well short of the long-term goal but which are nevertheless imperative in the meantime to reduce animal suffering. When I first heard of attempts in the United States to improve environmental conditions for nonhuman primates in laboratories I was rather skeptical. Having actually visited a primate research center in the United States and having witnessed the mental suffering of such creatures in small steel cages, I have come to see how essential and urgent it is to secure environmentally improved conditions.

Of course I would like to see not wider cages but empty cages, but until that day arrives it would be heartless not to do even the little that can be done to alleviate their misery. The same applies to many animals in zoos. Zoo animals suffer not only through captivity but because of their frequently barren, impoverished environment. There is no contradiction in seeking to improve the environmental conditions for zoo animals or primates in laboratories while simultaneously working for the abolition of both zoos and primate research centers.

Almost everyone in any position of political power can bring pressure to bear to improve the lot of animals, whether the individual be a local counselor voting on the use of land for circuses or hunting, or a senator dealing with national legislation. What is most urgent is that animal issues begin to occupy our legislative chambers, that the issue of animals is registered as a political issue requiring the exercise of political responsibility. In this regard I strongly endorse the decision of the U.K.'s Political Animal Lobby to donate one million pounds to the Labor Party. Some animal advocates have appeared incredulous that an animal society would take such a bold step, but in reality serious animal advocates have no choice: If one rejects violence and illegality (as I do), there is no alternative to embracing the political process. The strategy of progressive disengagement from injury to animals requires progressive—and mainstream—politicization.

Vital though this political work may be, working both professionally and pragmatically for each and every legislative reform, it is also important to understand that improvement for animals is not just a question of law. Not only is political power as currently conceived not the only center of power in our society (see point 6 below) but—more fundamentally—morality can never be about obedience to law *per se*. Law can help prevent the worst but it seldom by itself promotes the best. The law can and should provide minimum and basic standards for our treatment of animals but it cannot by itself transform our ethical understanding of them. That is why legislative advance—for all its desperate importance—is one, but only one, of the necessary processes of change.

One last point under this heading should perhaps be emphasized. Some commentators on the recent debate about hunting legislation in the United Kingdom have opposed legislation on the grounds that the government should not interfere in the "private lives" of individuals. It goes without saying that I cannot accept this view. Perhaps without realizing it, modern commentators are merely echoing the position of *The Times* editorial in 1800 which maintained that a bill to ban bullbaiting was misconceived since "whatever meddles with private personal disposition of a man's time is tyranny direct."[15] The contrary case should be advanced. If there is any moral basis for government at all, then it must be to defend the weak and the vulnerable who cannot defend themselves. Once seen in that light, the argument based on the supposed "civil liberty" of animal abusers is as hollow as that drawn from the supposed right of child abusers.

The sixth and last process concerns the conversion of ethical sensibility into successful capitalist enterprise. Some people, and I used to be one of them, think that the capitalist system is so rotten and so morally corrupt that it is inevitably the enemy of the vulnerable and the unprotected. I recall having written in my teens an article titled "Towards a Christian Socialist View of Animals," then published in the journal of the Christian Socialist Movement. I recall the argument to the effect that so long as animals are regarded as commodities, capitalist societies will always exploit them.[16]

I still hold to a socialist critique of capitalism, and it is surely true that so long as animals are regarded as commodities they will always be vulnerable under a free market system. But what I and many others have taken to be a sinister system (at least in its effects) may be more correctly described as a morally neutral one—one that can be utilized for good as well as bad ends. At the end of the day, commercial exploitation of animals flourishes because it makes money. The engine that drives all the principal fields of animal abuse in every area—from commercial horseracing to the production of new drugs—is capitalism.

So far all that capitalism has done—and that most effectively— is to harness the power of those who want to exploit animals. But all systems have their vulnerabilities, and the welcome vulnerability of the capitalist system from an animal rights perspective is precisely its dependency on the free market. Animal rights, I suggest, is a potentially huge market for contemporary capitalism.

Consider: If opinion polls are to be believed, there are already large majorities against the most mainstream abuse of animals in society today. For example, the national opinion poll commissioned by the *Daily Telegraph*[17] showed the following percentages who thought "It is not all right to . . ."

Hunt foxes to reduce numbers	52%
Feed farm animals with antibiotics	60%
Train animals for circuses	61%
Export veal calves to the continent	68%
Hunt foxes for recreation	72%
Raise "battery" hens	72%
Trap animals for fur	76%
Organize bullfights	77%
Keep veal calves in crates	78%
Organize bearbaiting	79%
Organize cock fights	79%

Even if slightly exaggerated, these figures represent nothing less than an intellectual revolution; they would have been inconceivable thirty, twenty, ten, even five years ago. The question then arises as to what mechanism there might be to translate these ethical majorities into practicing majorities.

I have already indicated how revolutionary the establishment of commercial ethical choice might be in the area of research and pharmaceutical products. But in the most basic area of all, namely food, the results would be no less revolutionary, arguably more so. When I became a vegetarian thirty years ago, it was in many ways practically difficult. Back then few people had even heard of vegetarians, and the alternative food available in health food stores, not to mention the usual fare in restaurants, was not at all attractive. It can be fairly said that being a vegetarian then involved some disadvantage. Finding the right food, appetizing enough to eat, was a daily challenge. Over the last thirty years, however, there has been a significant change. Vegetarian options—or at least some of them—are gradually beginning to compete, in taste, quality, and presentation, with their carnivorous rivals. What had dissuaded people—and to some extent still does—from becoming vegetarian is fast disappearing. But it hasn't disappeared entirely. Though some real progress has been made in terms of the production of mass, convenience veggie food, it has to be said that some packaged meat alternatives are still lackluster.

The point I'm trying to make is this: We do not yet have an even playing field. Veggie food, while often excellent, is not always so and, for those still stuck on "meat and two veg," prepackaged veggie alternatives are often not as cheap or, I'm told, as tasty. But it is important to realize how far we have already traveled. At long last major companies are competing for the veggie market with more attractively produced mass foods. Veggie food technology, while still in its infancy, is fast developing. And the day may yet come when excellent veggie food is as excellent, *and* cheap *and* convenient, as the alternative.

I believe the day will come when meat eating becomes the exception to the rule, when technology coupled with market capitalism outstrips and overtakes its rivals. What will the meat industry do when its fare is actually less tasty and more expensive? Such a scenario is not inconceivable in fifty or a hundred years. Remember: Necessity is the mother of invention. Inventive and enterprising capitalism will always follow the market—in fact, it has no alternative. When vegetarianism goes beyond its current ten percent mark and moves—as it surely will over the next ten years—upward to nearer twenty to thirty percent, the meat industry will find its products increasingly costly. As the balance begins to tilt I foresee a new market capitalism both responding to, and also helping to establish, a larger and larger vegetarian constituency. Science and business could lead the way in the development of ethical choice in medicine, food, and agriculture. What is needed is a scientific and capitalist sensibility in the service of a new ethical vision.

It will be noted that almost all my identified processes of change relate to institutions, whether they be commercial, political, or educational. This is because, in order to survive and prosper, animal-rights philosophy needs to be embodied in social life. Most people are creatures of habit, and institutions nurture and reinforce those habits. Sadly for the animals, many of our habits of life involve their exploitation. But it doesn't have to be that way. Our institutions, including our capitalist ones, merely reflect historic ways of thinking about animals. But as our ideas about animals change, so can our institutions. Doubtless it will be a long, uphill struggle, and personally I shall be dead and gone before the full force of these ideas finds social embodiment. But there will be change, and given the current and increasingly likely increase of consciousness, that change will be for the better.

16

Christ-like Ministry to Other Creatures

In the previous chapter I identified those processes of change which may reasonably give animal advocates some hope. Sometimes animal advocates can be the most despairing of all people (myself included). But, objectively, the advance of animal rights thinking is recognized even by those who work actively to oppose it. Thus, for example, one leading British newspaper noted for its implacable hostility to animal rights could begin one of its editorials with these words: "Political prediction is hazardous, but one safe forecast is possible: in the next decade, the issue of animal rights will become a growing national preoccupation."[1]

Some Christians may understandably be struck by how the processes of change described in the previous chapter appear largely secular. But that, I think, would be a mistake. I believe that these processes of change, from dark to light, are the work of the Holy Spirit within us in the world. And if that sounds strange we need to remind ourselves that God's Spirit is free and unchained. The Spirit is alive and abroad in creation whether or not the churches recognize it. And it is the Spirit working within all men and women of vision and goodwill, believers or nonbelievers, who is working out God's purpose throughout the scenes and turmoil of contemporary life. The world is not utterly cut adrift from the life of God, and if all our hope depended on the performance of the churches alone then we would surely be people without hope.

Most especially, the Spirit is the Spirit of life, and a dynamic, creative one at that. God has created a world that is subject to change: The world in which we live today has changed from the one in which we lived yesterday. Change is built into the very structure of God's creation. The Spirit works hiddenly, frequently mysteriously, within the creation that God has made. We should not therefore be surprised to find non-church people who have perceived the Gospel of life, and God's nonhuman life especially. I suspect that the Spirit is preparing a time of humbling for the churches. For so long, they have heard the Gospel of God's love and simply turned their backs. Now the churches will have to listen again to the Spirit in the world in order to rediscover the truth of their own Gospel.

In the meantime, can anything be expected of them? The question might, not unreasonably, be asked: "Where are the churches in all this?" Regrettably the answer has to be that they are still largely on the sidelines, indeed part of the problem rather than part of the solution. But it is easy, really too easy—as I indicated at the beginning of Part Two—to despair of the churches. Their failings of imagination and vision are for all to see. But Christians who believe that the Gospel creates community—indeed that it is God's will that Christian fellowship (*koinonia*) should be a sign and example to the world—cannot give up on the churches. And for one reason especially: God has not yet given up on them.

It is vital to grasp that while the work of the Holy Spirit is not dependent upon the churches, and while they frequently frustrate God's purposes, they can—sometimes even despite themselves—show signs of spiritual life and be a means of God's grace. I want to conclude therefore by suggesting ways in which they can assist this overall process of spiritual transformation. These concern three main areas: Worship, Gospel, and Ministry.

First, *worship*. Some people may not immediately see how Christian worship has a direct relevance to the future of animal liberation. In fact, it has a very simple one and it is this: Human beings are not God. In worshipping the Creator, we acknowledge that we are creatures. This all-too-simple idea has revolutionary implications in a society in which human needs, wants, aspirations, and benefits are thought to be the touchstones of all moral progress. We cannot, will not, be able to resist the claims of idolatry, at least in the long run, unless we are engaged in the worship of the one true God. I confess that I warm to the line of Malcolm Muggeridge that "savages prostrating themselves before a painted stone have always seemed to me to be nearer the truth than any Einstein or Bertrand Russell."[2] The very act of worship is an act of acknowledging a prior claim—that "the earth is the Lord's and the fullness thereof."[3]

The problem is, however, that the shape of a great deal of Christian worship remains firmly humanocentric, that is, human-centered. The very activity which should liberate us from preoccupation with ourselves more often than not actually feeds it. And the reason for this is simple: The world of creation, and animals especially, is invisible in our worship. We go on worshipping the Creator as though the rest of creation really wasn't there.

Of course, in one sense all worship is worship. At least it notionally directs our eyes behind the confines of our own species. But the shape, the language, and the structure of liturgy so often focus in on ourselves, as though we were the only species loved and cared for by God. Please don't misunderstand me: Of course it is important, even vital, that humans pray for forgiveness, repent of their sins, and receive spiritual nourishment and assurance in return. God does indeed renew us. But sometimes it is as though we want to worship God with closed ears to the wider praises of God's creatures.

Praising God is not just a human activity. At heart, of course, it is the Spirit who prays through us. But not only us. The Spirit alive in creation inspires the praise of the entire created order. How often we listen to those Psalms which speak so eloquently of the creation in praise, and then return to our own deeply self-centered worship of the same Creator God.

The test of worship is not only whether we are nourished and uplifted but also whether we have celebrated creation, enjoyed it (in the true sense of that word), appreciated it, felt more keenly for it, given thanks for it, and done this in cognizance that we—along with all creation—are sustained by the providential hand of God. It cannot be right to abstract ourselves from creation in the act of acknowledging our common Creator.

Years ago I used to think that Christian worship would in due course move inexorably toward a fuller sense of common creatureliness. But now I see that this can happen only by the transformation of liturgy itself: by bringing out more clearly—actually by *making visible*—that which current liturgy makes invisible. To this end, I have begun to compose, *inter alia*, prayers, litanies, eucharistic liturgies, and healing services which focus precisely on God's care for all creatures and correspondingly our duty to care for them also. My book *Animal Rites* may sound provocative but is really only an attempt to focus much of what has been lost in the history of liturgical development.[4]

In order to bring animals into worship we may well have to bring them into our worship. Years ago I produced for the RSPCA an Order of Service for Animal Welfare.[5] It is now in its fourth edition and serves countless parishes who every year make a point of worshipping with animals, literally inviting them into church, in order to remind Christians that animals too have one Heavenly Father. Having excluded animals for so long, bringing them in has obvious symbolic significance. Of course, for some parishes and clergy this service is a novelty and still treated with some disdain, even levity. But it can, and usually does, serve a vital purpose: to challenge the view that the God of Abraham, Isaac, Jacob, and Jesus is only concerned with the human species.

Sometimes, of course, these animals make a mess. But again it is a symbolic mess. Animals can and do make a mess of our self-centered worship: They give us, at best, a glimpse of creation in praise, a foretaste of the eternal Sabbath. "Animal services" or "animal rites" are now essential to restore the balance: to help enrich our sense of common creatureliness and to help us feel a sense of awe and wonder at the world God has made.

Some Christians respond fearfully to such developments, worried lest "animal worship" becomes just that: the worship of the creature rather than the Creator. But, in truth, the very reverse of idolatry is envisaged here. Until we can break free liturgically, in our worship, to embrace all God's creation, we will be doomed to a kind of parochialism in which we perpetuate human idolatry. This last point strikes me as very serious: We must not, dare not suppose, that God the Creator is solely preoccupied with the human species. Our interests are not *per se* God's interests. God is the Creator of all things: If we do not find ways of embodying this truth in our worship we will always run the risk of diminishing the act of divine worship itself. In short, we must revere life because of the Lord of life.

The symbolic neglect of fellow creatures in our church worship finds its corollary in a practical rejection of their actual presence in our places of worship as well. Years ago, a leading church newspaper ran a story of how under new British legislation the routine destruction of bats in churches would no longer be legal. Since bats often nest in church roofs, the legislation properly included church buildings since they provide one of the few remaining safe havens for a dwindling species. The resulting uproar, leading to nothing less than the establishment of a church group *opposed* to bat preservation, graphically revealed how theologically unenlightened about animals many Christians are.[6] Hardly any among the angry correspondents ever asked themselves whether some accommodation of other than human creatures might have some claim on Christian compassion. The issue is far from a trivial one. Many churches with large tracts of land, especially in country areas, have a unique opportunity to contribute to the preservation of threatened species. As it is, churches and cathedrals regularly arrange for the killing of thousands of "unwanted" species, especially pigeons, without ever considering non-lethal forms of control or indeed whether such control is actually necessary in the first place.[7]

The question must be posed: What kind of God are these Christians worshipping? A deity, it seems, wholly interested in preserving ecclesiastical buildings even at the expense of rendering some of God's other creatures extinct.

The second area I choose concerns *the Gospel* itself. If Christian worship is humanocentric, no less so is Gospel preaching. I have already argued in Chapter Two how the essence of this Gospel concerns nothing less than God's love for the entire creation. It would be difficult, however, for any serious or casual observer of Christian preaching to believe that this was actually the case, since so often key scriptural texts are given an entirely humanocentric emphasis. It is not that God so loves the world that is remembered, but rather God's love for humanity. Indeed, in more than twenty years of Christian ministry I cannot once recall a preacher preaching about God's love for the cosmos. The tragic truth is that God's inclusive loving has become a lost truth of Christian preaching.

The result has been to rarefy Christian teaching. I recall no less a person than C. S. Lewis writing that one of the earliest obstacles to his acceptance of Christianity was the apparent anomaly of God creating a vast universe but being practically concerned with only one small planet within it. Much contemporary proclamation of the Gospel is woefully parochial—tacitly assuming that the God who creates us is really only interested in the rest of creation as background or theater. But the effect of this tendency is not to make God more credible but less so. Why, after all, would God create an entire universe which was at heart a matter of sheer divine indifference?

Grasping then the inclusive and expansive nature of the Gospel—of the Good News of God's love—still remains a formidable challenge to the Church. One early work of apologetics I remember reading was called *Your God Is Too Small* by J. B. Phillips. Although obviously dated now, the main thrust of his argument—that we are always trying to limit God, to trim God to our size, to make God smaller than God necessarily is—has remained with me for years. It is the very "smallness" of Christian thought about the universe that helps make it so intellectually problematic. Of course, Christian preaching must adequately treat the great themes of human sinfulness and salvation, but it must never, absolutely never, suppose that God is exhausted in relationship to us—as if when one has treated these, and other human themes, this is all there is to be said. The God of the Christian Gospel is simply not reducible to human interests, themes, needs, or benefits.

But the challenge of the Gospel is not just an intellectual or theological one. It is also personal and practical, for the preaching of the Gospel of God's love is meant to challenge our lack of love as well as our constant desire to place ourselves and our wants at the center of the universe. It is astonishing that despite nearly two thousand years of Christian preaching Christians still seem so unskilled and parochial when it comes to the business of loving (including, of course, myself). But if this is so, it is so at least in part because we have defined human loving as the very center of all loving, to the exclusion of everything else. Of course, loving our fellow humans is desperately important, but it is not the only kind of loving possible. The love of God requires a love that begins to approximate God's own inclusive and expansive love. I like the lines of Van Gogh that if we want to know God we must love "many things":

> Love a friend, a wife, something, whatever you like, and you will be on the right way to know more about it . . . But one must love with a lofty and serious intimate sympathy, with strength, with intelligence, and one must always try to know deeper, better, and more. That leads to God, that leads to unwavering faith.[8]

I have yet to hear a Gospel sermon on the love of animals—a sermon, that is, which begins with a recognition of God's expansive and creative love and treats seriously how we can love animals, too, in a way that approximates God's love for them and for us. If the love and care of animals appears as an aberration or as an intrusion into normal Christian preaching, it is simply because we have failed to relate our faith to our full God-given potentialities for loving. If Christian clergy appear uncomfortable when members of their congregation speak of their love for other creatures, it is a sure sign that they themselves have a limited conception of the expansive love of God. I know that there are Christian leaders who can hardly speak of animals without smiling or raising a laugh, as though the whole notion that God loves other than human creatures is utterly foreign to the Christian Gospel. They are—to put it bluntly—embarrassed at any display of fellow-feeling or kinship with animals.

I select just one illustration. In a recent interview, the Bishop of London offered the view that "when our divine relationship is [so] weak . . . we find it easier to love whales or pandas rather than our fellow human beings."[9] Now it may be said that it is wrong to focus on one bishop's sleight-of-hand remark, but I suggest that is precisely what needs to be focused on: the sleight-of-hand manner in which issues about care for animals are treated by senior ecclesiastics. To be fair, the bishop was trying to make a serious point. It was that the breakdown of social, specifically family, relationships leads to, or is inseparable from, a decline in spiritual values. But what is so lamentable, even ludicrous, is the way in which he characterizes concern for animals as an inferior, even retrograde, form of spirituality. Another implication, equally unfortunate, is that we have to choose *between* humans and animals. At heart it's an either/or: pandas or people.

In fact, of course, we do not find it easier to love whales or pandas. Just for the record: Over one million, four hundred whales have been hunted to their deaths in the Southern Ocean alone this century. And for those who think all this has changed since the so-called moratorium, over sixteen thousand whales have been killed since 1986. Each death involves minimally half an hour of agony while the animals are harpooned, shot, or electrocuted. And pandas? For centuries these creatures have been ruthlessly hunted, so that there are now barely one and a half thousand left in the entire world. We are edging them off the planet. Very soon there will be no pandas left to love—except, of course, in the prisons of our own making where they are exhibited for entertainment. Love them? In truth, we have almost loved them to death.

The third and final area I choose concerns *Christian ministry*. It follows, of course, that a largely humanocentric form of worship in turn buttressed by a humanocentric preaching of the Gospel leads inexorably to a form of Christian ministry in which practical concern for animals is effectively excluded. Indeed, the very idea that caring for animals is a legitimate form of Christian ministry will strike many as distinctly oddball.

That we think it *is* oddball is itself significant. As indicated in Chapter 1, for Christian ministry to be truly Christ-like it must follow Christ. But Christ's ministry, according to Scripture, does not stop at Christians, even humankind. As the early Christians began to reflect on the significance of Christ's work, they were compelled not only to see it as the very work of God but also as nothing less than cosmic in scope. "For in him," writes Paul, "the complete being of God, by God's own choice, came to dwell. Through him God chose to reconcile the whole universe to himself, making peace through the shedding of blood upon the cross—to reconcile all things, whether on earth or in heaven, through him alone."[10]

It is a crying shame that so few Christians have taken these lines of Scripture at their face value and instead have variously maintained that these ideas represent transient cosmological wrapping. In fact, these words speak eloquently to us today when now more than ever Christians are aware of the interdependent nature of creation. We simply must abandon the idea that what happened in Christ is relevant and important for only one species in the universe God has created. Of course, Christ's ministry does have relevance for the human species, and that most centrally, because humans constitute the moral rot of the universe. Our sinfulness, wickedness, and violence call out to heaven for effective, remedial action. But while *centered* on humankind, God's ministry in Christ is not *limited* to one species alone. "All things" is the big biblical idea that we have still to learn—yes, "all things" in Christ.

This then is the basis for a contemporary Christian ministry to all creatures. Indeed, far from treasuring God's work of reconciliation in Christ as a possession of the human species alone, we should understand that the purpose of this reconciling work is to set us free—free, that is, to show forth and manifest that reconciling, healing ministry to other creatures. What is truly oddball and perverse is not ministry to all creatures but the reverse: the idea that while Christ's work is cosmic in scope, ours should be less so.

But what would a Christian ministry to creation look like? What would be its shape and structure? We need to focus on the word "reconciliation." To reconcile is to bring together that which was previously unreconciled. It goes without saying of course that humans are unreconciled—not only with God, but also with other creatures. Violence between species, and especially between the human and animal species, is the clearest sign of an unreconciled, fractured world. So much of our activity toward animals consists in divide and rule. For example: in hunting, coursing, and in terrier work especially, we help set creatures against each other. Dogs are bred and trained to chase and kill other creatures, notably foxes, mink, hares, and deer—bullbaiting, cockfighting, dog fighting all follow this same pattern. It is we who maximize and intensify the natural antipathy between creatures. Not only do we do this, but we compound it by enjoying it. As I have written elsewhere, "Sportsmen do not 'imitate' the cruelties of nature, they create them."[11]

This is but one example of our creation of a second, further order of violent, unredeemed nature. The churches could help us to see the essential perversity of human violence and cruelty. They could help liberate us from a limited conception of humanity as simply here for ourselves.

This is not a new thought. It is best expressed by the further idea of Paul that creation is in a state of childbirth, groaning in pain, awaiting deliverance.[12] And the new creation comes into being—according to this thought—principally through the activity of those already given the gift of reconciliation, namely human beings. It is we, in other words, who have the responsibility of demonstrating the reality of Christ's reconciliation by ourselves becoming reconciled to the rest of suffering creation.

I believe then that the Church must wake up to a new kind of ministry, not just to Christians or to human beings, but to the whole world of suffering creatures. It must be our human, Christian task to heal the suffering in the world. We must take every opportunity, even in things that appear small or insignificant, to lessen the burden of suffering on the animal world. Some Christian leaders—to their credit—have recognized this. Former Archbishop of Canterbury Donald Coggan said, "I am happy to follow the lead given to the Church some 150 years ago by the London vicar who called the meeting in 1824 which led to the RSPCA's foundation." And he continued, "There have always been, and still are, many churchmen, both lay and ordained, who have seen it as part of their Christian profession to work for animal welfare."[13]

Some may still press: How precisely can contemporary pastoral ministry become inclusive of animals? Again, that we think truly *pastoral* ministry can be exclusive of animals is significant. Think of the genesis of that term. To pastor, literally "to shepherd," arose out of a semi-agrarian context in which humans exercised their life in the care of animals, notably, of course, sheep. It is this idea of "caring for the flock" that has given us the contemporary model of pastoral care: the one who spends his or her life in the service of others. To the objection that the original shepherd may have cared for the flock but also killed them for food, it is worth recalling Jesus' own reported words that it is the "good" shepherd who not only desists from killing but actually "lays down his life" for the sheep.[14]

Once again we must challenge the idea that Christ-like care should be exclusive of animals. There is so much that local Christian communities can do to raise consciousness about animal suffering and to take the lead in devising practical programs for animal welfare. In accordance with the slogan "Think globally, act locally," church communities could become centers for action directed at exposing the abuse of animals in neighboring zoos, farms, research establishments, and, not least of all, the regular ill-treatment meted out to companion animals. By recapturing the original meaning of "pastoral," Christian communities could help challenge contemporary moral indifference.

It must be admitted, however, that the notion of "pastoral care," whether of humans or animals, has in a contemporary context become a rather tame notion. Stephen Pattison's book *Pastoral Care and Liberation Theology* has done us a service in helping us to see that individual care—if it is to be truly Christian—needs to be related to a liberating God who really does take sides with the poor, the vulnerable, and the oppressed. The God who enjoins us to care for the oppressed is the same God who will break all forms of oppression and injustice.[15] Indeed, the God who liberates is the one who has become the vulnerable. Pastoral care is the appropriate local means of appropriating God's own concern, but it must never become a palliative or an alternative to challenging unjust structures and institutions.

Some have indeed begun to see this, but most commonly only in relation to human subjects. "Open your mouth for the dumb, for the rights of all that are left desolate" says Proverbs 31:8. In commentary, one biblical scholar, Richard Bauckham, expounds the "special duty of those in power towards those who cannot secure rights for themselves." Indeed further, and in words which deserve to be savored:

But the principle of speaking out for the dumb requires continually renewed alertness to the needs of those who are *dumb*, who cannot speak for themselves, who in some cases may never be able to speak for themselves (the severely mentally handicapped, the very sick, the very old, and children, including the unborn), and who have not yet found those who can speak effectively for them. In a morally healthy democracy political parties and governments should be judged partly by their willingness to take up the cause of such groups, and the responsibility to see that they do is widely diffused among all who have some voice in the political process.[16]

The theology here strikes me as excellent, and what is more it has a precise christological grounding in the Christ-given paradigm of lordship expressed in service. But it will not have escaped the reader's attention that this paradigm properly, even supremely, applies to animal subjects as well. Animals are the "dumb" innocents *par excellence*: the ones who cannot speak for themselves, who suffer terribly at human hands and yet rely wholly on human representation to have any voice at all.

Hence we return to the underlying theme of the book: Preaching the Gospel has always a subversive aspect to it no matter how establishment Christians try to camouflage or submerge it. It is subversive because it necessarily speaks of a *different order* of justice and mercy than the one currently prevailing. This is true as much—or rather more—of animal concerns than it is of purely human ones. The Gospel breaks through into our thinking when we become convicted that our own judgments about what is right or wrong are self-serving, egoistical, or unjust, when we suddenly glimpse that from God's own perspective we stand condemned as mean and heartless. Communities of faith committed to a notion of repentance could help us feel sorrow for the cruelties we inflict on animals—indeed, not only to feel that sorrow (important as that is), but also to express it publicly, thereby helping us to change our lives.

But the Gospel hope has to be that the cries of the "dumb" *are* heard, that no matter how deaf human subjects may be, God hears the cries of the creatures. This is no idle conjecture. Indeed,

Christians fully cognizant of the justice of God should rather tremble at this future judgment. There is an old tradition, admittedly apocryphal, that at the last judgment the nonhuman creatures of the earth will be called in first by God to "give evidence" against each human being.[17] According to God's own reckoning, the last may become the first in a way hitherto almost undreamt of.

It is appropriate that we should end looking to the future. The Gospel is incomprehensible without an adequate sense of God's timescale and the belief in God's ultimate justice. Indeed, I am more and more sure that, without such a conviction, all moral striving will be seen as ultimately futile. Gospel hope in the future is not some optional extra to moral endeavor but its essential basis. For myself, I believe not only in this earth—and the beauty and value of all God's creatures within it—but also in the *new* earth—and all the redeemed creatures, both human and animal, that will belong to it. That our conception of heaven should be so devoid of other creatures is as lamentable as our limited conception of worship, Gospel, and ministry, indeed even more so. My own prayer is nowhere better expressed than by Henry Vaughan:

> O knowing, glorious Spirit, when
> Thou shalt restore trees, beasts and men,
> when thou shalt make all new again,
> destroying only death and pain,
> give him amongst Thy works a place,
> who in them loved and sought Thy face.[18]

Notes

Introduction: A Christian Credo for Animals

1. See Sydney Evans' moving meditation, "The Truth That Is in Christ Jesus—for Head, Heart and Hand," *Prisoners of Hope*, ed. Brian Horne and Andrew Linzey (Cambridge: Lutterworth Press, 1990), pp. 57–78.
2. John Clare, "I Am" in David Wright (ed.), *The Penguin Book of English Romantic Verse* (Harmondsworth, Middlesex: Penguin Books, 1968), p. 273.
3. C. S. Lewis and C. E. M. Joad, "On the Pains of Animals," *The Month*, vol. 3, no. 2 (February 1950), p. 98; see also my analysis, "C. S. Lewis's Theology of Animals," *Anglican Theological Review* (Winter 1998).
4. C. H. Spurgeon, "First Things First," *The Metropolitan Tabernacle Pulpit*, vol. xxxi (1885), p. 559. I am grateful to Adrian Hastings for this reference.
5. George MacLeod, cited in Ronald Ferguson, *George MacLeod: Founder of the Iona Community* (London: HarperCollins, 1990), p. 194.
6. Charles Péguy, cited by Ferguson, *George MacLeod*, p. 230.
7. Andrew Linzey, "Voyage to the Animal World," Foreword to Stephen H. Webb, *On God and Dogs: A Christian Theology of Compassion for Animals* (New York and Oxford: Oxford University Press, 1998), p. xi.
8. The U.S. edition of *Animal Theology* has been published by the University of Illinois Press (1995), the Spanish edition by Herder Editorial (1996), and the Italian edition by Edizioni Cosmopolis of Turin (1998). A chapter of the book is also published in the Swedish anthology, *Djur och manniskor*, ed. by Lisa Galmark (Nya Doxa, 1997).
9. In fact, I have also been centrally concerned with the rights of children. At my suggestion, in 1997, St. Xavier University, Chicago, organized and hosted the world's first multidisciplinary conference on the Rights of Children. My paper on "The Moral Priority of the Weak" will be published along with others in Brian Klug and Kathleen Alaimo (eds.), *Children as Equals? Exploring the Rights of the Child* (forthcoming).
10. A first draft of this confession was published in "A Gospel for Every Creature," *Expository Times*, vol. 107, no. 2 (November 1995), p. 48. I have also indicated the need for orthodox theology to take these starting points into account in my "Is Christianity Irredeemably Speciesist?" in Andrew Linzey and Dorothy Yamamoto (eds.), *Animals on the Agenda: Questions about Animals for Theology and Ethics* (London: SCM Press, 1998), pp. xvii–xviii. I am not the first to write a "confession" for animals. In the 1980s, two pioneering German pastors, Michael and Christa Blanke from Glauberg, wrote "A

Glauberg Confession for Animals" inviting church people and theologians to repent of their neglect and indifference to animals. For a copy, write to Pastors Michael and Christa Blanke, D 6475, Glauberg, Germany.

Chapter 1   Overview: Gospel Truths about Animals

A revised version of a paper originally presented to a conference titled "Not a Sparrow Falls" arranged by Christian Impact in London and published in *Third Way* (May 1995).

1. See Genesis 1:27–30.
2. Colossians 3:9 f and 12.
3. Mark 2:16.
4. Lord Shaftesbury, letter dated April 30, 1881, cited by Roberta Kalechofsky in *Between the Species: A Journal of Ethics*, vol. 6, no. 3 (Summer 1990), p. 160; also cited and discussed in Andrew Linzey, *Animal Theology* (London: SCM Press, 1994), p. 36.
5. Frances Power Cobbe, *In Memoriam: The Late Earl of Shaftesbury, K.G., First President of the Victoria Street Society* (London: Victoria Street Society, 1885); cited and discussed in Molly Baer Kramer and Andrew Linzey, "Vivisection," in Paul Barry Clarke and Andrew Linzey (eds.), *Dictionary of Ethics, Theology and Society* (London and New York: Routledge, 1996), p. 872.
6. Mark 1:13.
7. Matthew 21:1–7.
8. Matthew 12:10 ff.
9. Luke 12:6 and 27.
10. Luke 9:58.
11. John 1:36.
12. Colossians 1:19 f.
13. Romans 8:18–24a.
14. Michael Ramsey, cited and discussed in John V. Taylor, *The Christlike God* (London: SCM Press, 1992), p. 100.
15. C. S. Rodd (editorial), *Expository Times*, vol. 106, no. 1 (October 1994). However, I am glad to acknowledge my indebtedness to Rodd for a perceptive and insightful review. Under his editorship, *Expository Times* has demonstrated a commendable openness to issues about theology and animals.
16. Karl Barth, *Dogmatics in Outline* [1949], trans. by G. T. Thomson (London: SCM Press, 1968), p. 66.

Chapter 2   For God So Loved the World

A reworked version of an address originally given at a Service for Animal Welfare at Salisbury Cathedral and published in *Between the Species: A Journal of Ethics*, vol. 6, no. 1 (Winter 1990).

1. E. P. Evans, *The Criminal Prosecution and Capital Punishment of Animals* [1906] (London: Faber and Faber, 1987), Appendix N, pp. 304–5.

2. Aquinas, cited by Evans, *The Criminal Prosecution*, pp. 54–5.

3. See, for example, Henry Davis: "Animals have no rights; they can give us nothing freely nor understand our claims. We have no duties of charity or justice toward them, but as they are God's creatures, we have duties *concerning them* and the right use we make of them. In the treatment of animals we may not give way to rage or impatience, nor invade our neighbor's right of ownership of them . . ." *Moral and Pastoral Theology*, vol. II, *Commandments of God: Precepts of the Church* (London: Sheed and Ward, 5th edition, 1946), p. 258, my emphases; extract in Andrew Linzey and Tom Regan (eds.), *Animals and Christianity: A Book of Readings* (London: SPCK and New York: Crossroad, 1989), pp. 130–31. This view may—but only may— have been modified (at least in respect of duties) by the *Catholic Catechism*; see discussion in chapter 7.

4. Aquinas, *Summa Contra Gentiles*, in Anton C. Pegis (trans.), *Basic Writings of St. Thomas Aquinas* (New York: Random House, 1945), vol. II, pp. 220–24; extract in P. A. B. Clarke and Andrew Linzey (eds.), *Political Theory and Animal Rights* (London and Winchester, Mass.: Pluto Press, 1990), p. 10.

5. Sydney Evans, *Apostolate and the Mirrors of Paradox*, ed. by Andrew Linzey and Brian Horne (Oxford: SLG Press, 1996), p. 8.

6. Fyodor Dostoevsky, *The Brothers Karamazov*, trans. with an introduction by David Magarshack, vol. I (Harmondsworth, Middlesex: Penguin Books, 1958), p. 375.

7. Ibid, p. 376.

8. Martin Luther King, *The Trumpet of Conscience* (London: Hodder & Stoughton, 1968), p. 89. I gladly acknowledge my indebtedness to King for his inspiration.

9. I make the same point and in much the same words in my *Animal Theology*, pp. 149–50.

10. See Andrew Linzey and Tom Regan (eds), *Compassion for Animals: Readings and Prayers* (London: SPCK, 1988) for extracts from the Bible, and the writings of theologians, saints, and poets on the theme of animal welfare.

11. W. H. Auden, "September 1939," in *The English Auden*, ed. by E. Mendleson (London: Faber and Faber, 1977), p. 245.

Chapter 3   Unfinished and Unredeemed Creation

A revised version of a paper originally given to a consultation of ecologists and animal advocates titled "Ethical Relations with Other Creatures" in Arkansas, sponsored by the Center for Respect for Life and the

Environment of the HSUS (Humane Society of the United States) and published in *EcoTheology* (Winter 1998).

1. "The Acts of Philip" in J. K. Elliott (ed.), *The Apocryphal New Testament* (Oxford: The Clarendon Press, 1993), pp. 515–16. Elliott has modernized the earlier translation originally in Montague Rhodes James (ed.), *The Apocryphal New Testament* (Oxford: The Clarendon Press, 1924), VIII, pp. 446–47 and 438–39.
2. James, p. 438.
3. Rachel Trickett, "Imagination and Belief," in A. E. Harvey (ed.), *God Incarnate: Story and Belief* (London: SPCK, 1981), p. 39. See also Brian Horne, "Seeing with a Different Eye: Religion and Literature," in Andrew Linzey and Peter J. Wexler (eds.), *Heaven and Earth: Essex Essays in Theology and Ethics* (London: Churchman Publishing, 1986), pp. 121–24. I am indebted to Horne's discussion of Trickett which I have used in connection with other apocryphal material about Jesus and animals in Andrew Linzey and Dan Cohn-Sherbok, *After Noah: Animals and the Liberation of Theology* (London: Cassell, 1997), see esp. chapters 4 and 5.
4. Trickett, pp. 38–9.
5. James, *The Apocryphal New Testament*, p. 438.
6. Richard Cartwright Austin, *Beauty of the Lord: Awakening the Senses* (Atlanta: John Knox Press, 1988), pp. 196–97. See also my critique, "The Case Against the Christian Hunter" in *Epworth Review*, vol. 20, no. 2 (May 1993) pp. 22–30; also in my *Animal Theology*, chapter 7.
7. Matthew Fox and Jonathon Porritt, "Green Spirituality" (a dialogue) in *Creation Spirituality*, vol. VII, no. 3, (May/June 1991), pp. 14–15. Also cited and discussed in my *Epworth Review* article.
8. See, for example, Francis Bridger, "Ecology and Eschatology: A Neglected Dimension" in *Tyndale Bulletin*, vol. 41, no. 2 (1990), pp. 290–301.
9. Luther, *Lectures on Romans*, ed. by Wilhelm Pauck, Library of Christian Classics, vol. XV (London: SCM Press, 1961), p. 237.

Chapter 4   The Rights of God's Creatures

An adapted version of an article that first appeared in the *Christian Century*, vol. 108, no. 28 (October 9, 1991).

1. Louis Sullivan, cited in the *National Catholic Reporter*, vol. 27, no. 6 (November 30, 1990), p. 4.
2. William Henry Holcombe, cited in David Brian Davis, *Slavery and Human Progress* (New York and Oxford: Oxford University Press, 1986), p. 23.
3. George Fox, cited in William C. Braithwaite, *The Second Period of Quakerism* (1919), p. 270; cited and discussed in Keith Thomas, *Man and*

the Natural World: Changing Attitudes in England 1500–1800 (Harmondsworth, Middlesex: Penguin Books, 1984), p. 43.

4. P. Palazzini (ed.), *Dictionary of Moral Theology*, compiled by F. Roberti, trans. by H. J. Yannone (London: Burns and Oates, 1962), p. 73.

5. Donald Coggan, Presidential Message to the Annual General Meeting of the RSPCA, RSPCA *Today*, no. 22 (July 1977), p. 1.

6. Robert Runcie, "Address at the Global Forum of Spiritual and Parliamentary Leaders on Human Survival," April 11, 1988, pp. 13–14; original emphases.

7. Pope John Paul II, *Sollicitudo Rei Socialis*, Encyclical Letter (London: Catholic Truth Society, 1988), par. 34, pp. 64–65.

8. *National Catholic Reporter*.

9. John Selwyn Gummer reported in the *Daily Telegraph*, May 3, 1990.

10. Karl Barth, *Church Dogmatics*, vol. III/I, ed. by G. W. Bromiley and T. F. Torrance (Edinburgh: T & T Clark, 1958), p. 208.

11. Lloyd Billingsley, "Save the Beasts, not the Children? The Dangerous Premises of the Animal-Rights Crusade," *Eternity* (February 1985), pp. 35–36. Published by Evangelical Ministries Inc., Philadelphia.

12. I also make this point and in more detail in *Animal Theology*, pp. 33–35.

13. Psalm 36:6, cited and discussed by Karl Barth, *Church Dogmatics*, III/I, p. 181.

14. I have subjected Singer's "equality of interests view" to sustained critique in my *Animal Theology*, chapter 2. I propose that his "Equality paradigm" should be replaced by a christologically based "Generosity paradigm."

15. See Andrew Linzey, *Christianity and the Rights of Animals* (London: SPCK and New York: Crossroad, 1987), chapter 5: "The Theos-Rights of Animals."

Chapter 5 Animals as a Case of Theological Neglect

Originally composed in response to Archbishop John Habgood's article in *The Times* ("Claiming animal 'rights' devalues cases of basic human need," February 11, 1995, p. 9) and published as a Guest Editorial in *Reviews in Religion and Theology*, no. 3 (August 1995).

1. Habgood, "Claiming Animal 'Rights.'"

2. Ibid.

3. Paul Johnson, "No Animals Have Rights, but Human Beings Have Duties to Them," *The Spectator*, April 29, 1995.

4. Hugh Montefiore, "Animals Have No Rights, but They Deserve Our Care," *Church Times*, May 5, 1995.

5. The RSPCA Minutes record how the "establishment of societies to prevent cruelty to animals has brought forth a strong public sense

of duty towards children, who, like domestic animals, are defenseless against the ill-treatment of persons having charge of them," and goes on to record examples of how SPCA members helped support and fund pioneering anti-cruelty societies in Liverpool and New York, *The Animal World* (September 1884), p. 131. I am grateful to Olive Martyn, librarian of the RSPCA, and Nick Mays, archivist of the NSPCC, for the historical documentation. For a historical overview see David Owen, *English Philanthropy*, 1660–1960 (London: Oxford University Press, 1965).
6. See, for example, my critique in *Christianity and the Rights of Animals*, pp. 94–8.

Chapter 6   Animal Rights as Religious Vision

First presented as a paper to a conference on "Faiths and the Environment" arranged by the Center for Inter-Faith Dialogue at Middlesex University, and subsequently published in the Conference Papers under the same title by Middlesex University in 1996 and edited by Christopher Lamb.

1. John Austin Baker, *The Foolishness of God* (London: Darton, Longman and Todd, 1970), p. 406.
2. Andrew Rowan, cited in Tom Regan, "Foreword," *Political Theory and Animal Rights*, p. ix.
3. William Temple in F. A. Iremonger, *William Temple, Archbishop of Canterbury: His Life and Letters* (London and Oxford: Oxford University Press, 1948), pp. 18–19.
4. Raymond (R. G.) Frey, *Interests and Rights: The Case Against Animals* (Oxford: The Clarendon Press, 1977), preface.
5. "Animal Wrongs" (lead article), *The Trumpet Call*, Journal of the Peniel Pentecostal Church, 17th Issue (1995), pp. 1–18.
6. John R. W. Stott argues that the animal-rights movement is a form of animal worship, see "Christians and Animals," *Christianity Today*, 22, 10 (February 1978), pp. 33–39.
7. From SB 8.38, Abu Hurayra, cited in Neal Robinson (ed.), *The Sayings of Muhammad* (London: Duckworth, 1991), p. 49.
8. The notion of *ahimsa*, originally an emphasis of the Jain and Buddhist traditions, was translated in modern times by Gandhi as "non-violence"; it provides for those traditions and Hinduism an expression of their common respect for all life, see R. C. Zaehner, *Hinduism* (Oxford: Oxford University Press, 1966), pp. 70 and 170. For an account of Gandhi's spiritual quest and his commitment to vegetarianism, see M. K. Gandhi, *An Autobiography* (Ahmedabad, India: Navajivan Publishing House, 1929), pp. 41 ff.
9. O. P. Dwivedi, "Satyagraha for Conservation: Awakening the Spirit of Hinduism" in J. Ronald Engel and Joan Gibb Engel (eds.), *Ethics*

of Environment and Development: Global Challenge, International Response (London: Bellhaven Press, 1990), pp. 210–12.

10. From SB 8.11, Abu Hurayra, cited in Robinson, *The Sayings of Muhammad*, p. 48.

11. See Richard H. Schwartz, "Tsa'ar Ba'alei Chayim—Judaism and Compassion for Animals" in Roberta Kalechofsky (ed.), *Judaism and Animal Rights: Classical and Contemporary Responses* (Marblehead, Mass.: Micah Publications, 1992), pp. 59–70.

12. R. C. Zaehner (ed. and trans.), *The Bhagavad Gita* (Oxford: Oxford University Press, 1969), chapter XII, 13, p. 89 and commentary p. 329.

13. E. A. Burtt (ed.), *The Teachings of the Compassionate Buddha* (New York: New American Library, 1955), "The Bodhisattva's Vow of Universal Redemption," pp. 133–34.

14. Al-Hafiz B. A. Masri, *Islamic Concern for Animals* (Petersfield: The Athene Trust, 1987).

15. Richard H. Schwartz, *Judaism and Vegetarianism* (Marblehead, Mass.: Micah Publications, 1988).

16. Roberta Kalechofsky, *Judaism and Animal Rights*, see esp. "The Social and Medical Antecedents to the Nazi Concentration Camps," pp. 282–90; see also her *Autobiography of a Revolutionary: Essays on Animal and Human Rights* (Marblehead, Mass.: Micah Publications, 1991).

17. Philip Kapleau, *To Cherish All Life: A Buddhist Case for Becoming Vegetarian* (New York: Harper & Row, 1982).

18. Henry Beston, *The Outermost House: A Year of Life on the Great Beach of Cape Cod* (Harmondsworth, Middlesex: Penguin, 1928), p. 25. I am grateful to Brian Klug for this reference.

Chapter 7   Why Church Teaching Perpetuates Cruelty

An expanded version of an article originally published in *The AV*, the Journal of the American Anti-Vivisection Society (October 1994).

1. *The Catholic Catechism* (London: Geoffrey Chapman, 1994), paras. 2415–18, pp. 516–17.

2. *Sollicitudo Rei Socialis*.

3. *Catechism*, par. 353, p. 81.

4. Aquinas, "Whether irrational creatures ought to be loved out of charity," *Summa Theologica* (New York: Benzinger Brothers, 1918), Question 65.3; extract in *Political Theory and Animal Rights*, pp. 103–5.

5. I develop this same point in Andrew Linzey and Dan Cohn-Sherbok, *After Noah*, p. 131.

6. For this same point and also an analysis of the significance of the religious opposition to vivisection, see Molly Baer Kramer and Andrew Linzey, "Vivisection" in *Dictionary of Ethics, Theology and Society*, p. 871.

7. Martin Buber cited in H. A. Williams, *Some Day I'll Find You: An Auto-biography* (London: Mitchell Beazley, 1982), p. v.

Chapter 8   The Christ-like Innocence of Animals

A revised version of an article originally published in the *Catholic Herald*, May 20, 1994.

1. There is a lengthy discussion of the positive teaching and example of the saints about animals in *After Noah*, chapters 4 and 5.
2. John Henry Newman, "The Crucifixion" |1842| Sermon X, *Parochial and Plain Sermons* (London: Rivingtons, 1868), pp. 133–45. I am grateful to James Gaffney for this reference, and for his ground-breaking essay, "Can Catholic Morality Make Room for Animals?" in Andrew Linzey and Dorothy Yamamoto (eds.), *Animals on the Agenda*.
3. Newman, p. 138.
4. C. S. Lewis, *The Problem of Pain* (London: Geoffrey Bles, 1940), p. 117.
5. Opponents of vivisection during that period included E. B. Nicholson (librarian of the Bodleian), H. P. Liddon (Bishop of Oxford), Lewis Carroll (Charles L. Dodgson), and John Ruskin. Indeed Ruskin resigned his Chair of Fine Art following the vote—in his own words—"endowing vivisection in the University." For a brief account of the controversies at Oxford about animals, see my publication *Ethical Concern for Animals* (Mansfield College, Oxford, 1992); also the remarkable cartoon featuring the vivisection debate in Paul Weindling, "The University's Contribution to the Life Sciences and Medicine" in John Prest (ed.), *The Illustrated History of Oxford University* (Oxford: Oxford University Press, 1993), p. 282.
6. *Veritatis Splendor*, p. 124.
7. See, for example, the recent studies by Arnold Arluke and Carter Luke, "Understanding Cruelty to Animals," pp. 183–93; Frank R. Anscione, Claudia V. Weber, and David S. Wood, "The Abuse of Animals and Domestic Violence," pp. 205–18; and Carol D. Raupp, Mary Barlow, and Judith A. Oliver, "Perceptions of Family Violence: Are Companion Animals in the Picture?" pp. 219–37—all in *Society and Animals*, vol. 5, no. 3 (1997). For pioneering work on humane education and the links between child and animal cruelty, contact The Latham Foundation, Latham Plaza Building, Clement and Schiller Streets, Alameda, California 94501.
8. Washington Humane Society poster reproduced in *Society and Animals*, p. 235.
9. His classic work is, of course, *An Essay on the Development of Christian Doctrine* |1845|, ed. J. M. Cameron (Harmondsworth, Middlesex: Penguin Books, 1973).

Chapter 9 Overview: The Dream Dreams Us

Originally given as a keynote address to the Annual Conference of the Humane Society of the United States at Houston, Texas, and published in *Between the Species: A Journal of Ethics* (Spring 1991).

1. Martin Luther King, *Why We Can't Wait* (New York: Bantam Books, 1969), p. 43. There appear to be various—interestingly different— accounts of what King actually said. The account I have chosen is King's own edited version.
2. Information from "Prospectus of the SPCA," RSPCA *Records*, vol II (1823–26), pp. 203–4. I am grateful to the librarian of the RSPCA for a copy of this document. See also A. W. Moss, *Valiant Crusade: The History of the Royal Society for the Prevention of Cruelty to Animals* (London: Cassell, 1961), p. 23.
3. I say "first *national* society" because the Liverpool Society for Preventing Wanton Cruelty to Animals was founded in 1809, although it appears to have been rather short-lived; see Moss, pp. 20–21.
4. "Prospectus," pp. 198–99.
5. Ibid.
6. See Moss, *Valiant Crusade*, pp. 48–67.
7. "Prospectus," p. 201.
8. "Prospectus," p. 201; my emphases.
9. RSPCA Minute Book, no 1, pp. 38, 40–41. Cited in James Turner, *Reckoning with the Beast: Animals, Pain and Humanity in the Victorian Mind* (Baltimore, Md.: The Johns Hopkins University Press, 1980), p. 154. Turner argues that this declaration was made principally to exclude "[Lewis] Gompertz's Jewishness," but this overlooks the deliberate association of the Society with Christianity, which is implicit in the founding documents.
10. See Edward G. Fairholme and Wesley Pain, *A Century of Work for Animals: The History of the RSPCA, 1824–1924* (London: John Murray, 1924), esp. pp. 49–64.
11. George Bernard Shaw, cited in Hesketh Pearson, *Bernard Shaw: His Life and Personality* (London: The Reprint Society, 1948), inside page.
12. William Godwin, *Enquiry Concerning Political Justice and Its Influence on Modern Morals and Happiness* [1798] (Harmondsworth, Middlesex: Penguin Books, 1976), pp. 401–2. This section is reprinted in *Political Theory and Animal Rights*, pp. 132–35.
13. Cited in David L. Lewis, *Martin Luther King: A Critical Biography* (London: Allen Lane, 1976), p. 191.
14. The line was originally passed on to my wife (through me) from Colman McCarthy of the *Washington Post*. I acknowledge my debt to Colman's perspicacity.
15. George Bernard Shaw, "Killing for Sport" [March, 1914] in *Prefaces by Bernard Shaw* (London: Constable, 1934), p. 139.

16. I make this point in "The Place of Animals in Creation—A Christian View," in Tom Regan (ed.), *Animal Sacrifices: Religious Perspectives on the Use of Animals in Science* (Philadelphia: Temple University Press, 1986), p. 140.
17. Romans 3:23.
18. Again I make the same point in my contribution to *Animal Sacrifices*, p. 140.
19. Albert Schweitzer, *Civilization and Ethics*, trans. C. T. Campion, (London: Allen and Unwin, 1967), p. 221.
20. See Fairholme and Pain, *A Century of Work for Animals*, p. 64.
21. Gandhi, cited in Lewis, *Martin Luther King*, p. 210.
22. Isaiah 11:6–9.
23. For extracts from these biblical books, see *Animals and Christianity: A Book of Readings*.
24. Edward Buffet, *History of the ASPCA*, vol VII, *Bergh's War on Vested Cruelty* (ASPCA unpublished manuscript, c. 1924), no page number. I am grateful to Bernard Unti for his generous assistance in obtaining a copy of the chapter on "Ecclesiastical Relations," as well as his pioneering work on the history of the animal-protection movement in the United States.
25. Details of the major pronouncements by the churches are found in an appendix to *Christianity and the Rights of Animals*, pp. 150–58. The Report to the World Council of Churches titled "Liberating Life" is reproduced as an appendix to Charles Pinches and Jay B. McDaniel (eds.), *Good News for Animals? Christian Approaches to Animal Well-Being* (New York: Orbis Books, 1993), pp. 235–52.
26. Extract in David J. Garrow, *Bearing the Cross: Martin Luther King Jr. and the Southern Christian Leadership Conference* (London: Jonathan Cape, 1988), p. 621.
27. Martin used this phrase at the end of his speech in Los Angeles in 1963; see Lewis, *Martin Luther King*, p. 210.

Chapter 10   Moral Means to Moral Ends

An expanded version of an article that first appeared in *The Times Higher*, December 23, 1994.

1. See "Beauty Firms Fight Back on Animal Tests," *Guardian*, August 4, 1989, p. 22.
2. For a classic statement of this position, see Tom Regan, *The Case for Animal Rights* (Berkeley, Calif.: University of California Press, 1993).
3. I have read some "direct action" literature in the United States to the effect that activists must risk only "minimal" harm to humans or animals in the course of their attacks. Needless to say, I cannot agree that this is morally acceptable. Indeed, such a view is utterly

inconsistent with an informed animal-rights position which must logically oppose *any* risk of harm—minimal or otherwise—to innocent subjects, human or animal.

4. See *New Life for Animals* (London: Labor Party, 1997). Among the far-reaching policies proposed are: the phasing out of battery cages, a royal commission on animal experimentation, the abolition of fur farming, maximum journey time for animals in transit, improved standards for zoos, increased protection for wildlife, and a Europe-wide embargo on trapping exotic birds.

5. Martin Luther King, *Trumpet of Conscience*, p. 89.

Chapter 11   Toward Cruelty-Free Science

Originally an address given to an International Conference on Ethical Science held in Helsingborg, Sweden, and published in *International Animal Action*, Bulletin of the International Association Against Painful Experiments on Animals, no. 38 (Spring 1997).

1. Susan E. Lederer, *Subjected to Science: Human Experimentation before the Second World War* (Baltimore and London: The Johns Hopkins University Press, 1995).

2. Ibid, pp. xiv and xv.

3. Ibid, p. 123.

4. Ibid, pp. 100 f.

5. Lewis Carroll (Charles L. Dodgson), *Some Popular Fallacies about Vivisection* (printed for private circulation, Oxford, June 1875), see esp. pp. 14–16.

6. C. S. Lewis, *Vivisection* (Boston: New England Anti-Vivisection Society, 1947), p. 6.

7. R. G. Frey, *Rights, Killing and Suffering: Moral Vegetarianism and Applied Ethics* (Oxford: Blackwell, 1983), p. 113.

8. Helsinki Declaration [1964, 1975], article 1.5, cf. article III.4, see the *Proposed International Guidelines for Biochemical Research Involving Human Subjects*, A Joint Project of the World Health Organization and the Council for Organizations of Medical Sciences (Geneva, 1982), p. 22, paras 1 f; and my discussion in *Animal Theology*, pp. 111–13. I am grateful to John Finnis for this reference.

9. The Labor Government has refused to issue anymore licences for cosmetic experiments since its election in May 1997 and the "three companies holding [the remaining] four licenses . . . agreed to stop the tests following approaches by the Government," Shenai Raif, PA News, November 6, 1997.

10. MORI Opinion Poll on animal welfare, the *Daily Telegraph*, August 8, 1995.

11. C. S. Lewis, *Vivisection*, p. 3.

Chapter 12   Brave New Unnatural World

Originally based on an address given at Burford Church, Oxfordshire, filmed as part of BBC 2's program on the genetic engineering of farm animals, titled "One Man's Meat" on May 9, 1995, and published in *GenEthics News*, issue 6 (June 1995).

1. For a first-rate review of current developments and their scientific and ethical implications, see David King, *Review of the Literature on Genetic Manipulation* (forthcoming). Two excellent publications which regularly monitor, explain, and criticize new developments are *Splice*, magazine of the Genetics Forum (5–11 Worship Street, London EC2A 2BH), and *GenEthics News* (PO Box 6313, London N16 0DY).
2. "One Man's Meat" program.
3. Joyce D'Silva and Peter Stevenson, *Modern Breeding Technologies and the Welfare of Farm Animals*, p. 8.
4. Andrew Linzey, "Created not Invented: A Theological Critique of Patenting Animals," *Crucible*, Quarterly Journal of the Board for Social Responsibility of the Church of England (April/June 1993), p. 68.
5. David Bradshaw, "Introduction" to Aldous Huxley, *Brave New World* |1932| (London: HarperCollins, 1994), p. 7.
6. Ibid., p. 6.
7. In *Animal Theology*, I discuss the views of one pre-Nazi, Christian eugenicist, Percy Gardner, pp. 151 f.
8. C. S. Lewis, "Preface" to *That Hideous Strength* |1945| in *The Cosmic Trilogy* (London: Pan Books, 1989), p. 353.
9. Ibid, pp. 386–87.
10. C. S. Lewis, *The Abolition of Man* |1943| (London: HarperCollins, 1978), p. 37.
11. Ibid, p. 35.
12. W. B. Adams, *Journal of the Society of Arts*, vol. v (March 27, 1857), p. 293. I am grateful to Peter J. Wexler for this reference.
13. See Fran Abrams, "Church Invests in Gene Science," *Independent*, July 18, 1997.
14. Biotechnology and the European Public Concerted Action Group, "Europe Ambivalent on Biotechnology," ("Commentary"), *Nature*, vol. 387 (June 26, 1997), p. 847. I am grateful to Jacky Turner for this reference.
15. David Bradshaw, "Introduction," p. 9, and in "Foreword" by Huxley, *Brave New World*, p. 3.
16. C. S. Lewis, *The Abolition of Man*, see the appendix on "Illustrations of the Tao," pp. 49–59. Lewis also writes, "The regenerate science which I have in mind would not do even to minerals and vegetables what modern science threatens to do to man himself . . .

While studying the *It* it would not lose what Martin Buber calls the *Thou*-situation," p. 47; original emphases.

Chapter 13   Ethical Objections to Cloning

A revised version of an article originally published in the *Bulletin of Medical Ethics*, no. 131 (September 1997).

1. See, *inter alia*, Robin McKie, "A Clone Again, Naturally," Observer essay, *Observer*, March 9, 1996; Colin Tudge, "In Whose Interest?," *Independent*, March 11, 1996; Stephen Clover, "Relax Everyone: They Can't Clone Saddam Hussein," *The Times*, February 28, 1997; Rupert Cornwell and Charles Arthur, "Now Monkeys Get the Cloning Treatment," *Independent*, March 3, 1997; John Grace, "Man or Mouse?," *Guardian*, March 4, 1997.

2. Among the major works are: Stephen R. L. Clark, *The Moral Status of Animals* (Oxford: Clarendon Press, 1977); Mary Midgley, *Animals and Why They Matter* (Athens, Ga.: University of Georgia Press, 1983); S. F. Sapontzis, *Morals, Reason and Animals* (Philadelphia: Temple University Press, 1987); Rosemary Rodd, *Biology, Ethics and Animals* (Oxford: Clarendon Press, 1990); James Rachels, *Created from the Animals: The Moral Implications of Darwinism* (Oxford: Oxford University Press, 1990).

3. David DeGrazia, *Taking Animals Seriously: Mental Life and Moral Status* (Cambridge: Cambridge University Press, 1996), p. 284.

4. See K. H. S. Campbell, J. McWhir, W. A. Ritchie, and I. Wilmut, "Sheep Cloned by Nuclear Transfer from a Cultured Cell Line," *Nature*, 380, pp. 64–66 (1996), and the report "Giant Sheep Clones Worry Scientists," *The Sunday Times*, March 10, 1996, pp. 1–2.

5. *The Sunday Times*, p. 1.

6. I. Wilmut, A. E. Schnleke, J. McWhir, A. J. Kind, and K. H. S. Campbell, "Viable Offspring Derived from Fetal and Adult Mammalian Cells," *Nature*, 385, pp. 810–13 (1997).

7. Science and Technology Committee, *The Cloning of Animals from Adult Cells*, House of Commons (London: HMSO, 1997), vol. I, p. vi.

8. The distinction is defended in Andrew Linzey, "The Place of Animals in Creation—A Christian View," in *Animal Sacrifices*, pp. 115–48.

9. For two reports of these various techniques and the welfare implications, see Joyce D'Silva and Peter Stevenson, *Modern Breeding Technologies and the Welfare of Farm Animals*, and Tim O'Brien, *Gene Transfer and the Welfare of Animals*, pp. 1–22 (Petersfield, Hampshire: Compassion in World Farming, 1995).

10. It is useful to compare the warnings of Ruth Harrison's *Animal Machines* (London: Vincent Stuart, 1964) with Andrew Johnson's more recent *Factory Farming* (Oxford: Basil Blackwell, 1991).

11. John Habgood, "Send Out the Clones," *Observer*, March 2, 1997, p. 27.
12. Ibid.
13. See, for example, Bernard E. Rollin, *The Unheeded Cry: Animal Consciousness, Animal Pain and Science* (Oxford: Oxford University Press, 1989), and the up-to-date empirical documentation in DeGrazia, *Taking Animals Seriously*, esp. chapters 2–7.
14. Habgood, "Send Out the Clones."
15. Peter Street, text of "Horizon" program, "Fast Life in the Food Chain," 1992; cited and discussed in D'Silva and Stevenson, *Modern Breeding Technologies*, p. 17.
16. For example the attack on religious perspectives by Richard Dawkins, "Dolly and the Cloth-heads," *Independent*, March 3, 1997.
17. Science and Technology Committee, *The Cloning of Animals*, pp. vi–viii.
18. Ibid., p. xiv.
19. Prince of Wales, "Address to the Soil Association," *Independent*, September 20, 1996.
20. *Christianity and the Rights of Animals*, "The Theos-Rights of Animals" (chapter 5), pp. 68–98.
21. The argument is pursued at some length in *After Noah*, pp. 118 f.

Chapter 14   Bishops Say No to Fur

1. *Harvesting Wildlife in the Canadian North: A Question of Cultural Survival of Aboriginal Peoples*, a joint statement of social concern by Roman Catholic and Anglican Bishops in Northern Canada (March 1986); extract in *Animals and Christianity*, pp. 167–70.
2. Andrew Linzey (ed.), *Cruelty and Christian Conscience: Bishops Say No to Fur* (Nottingham: Lynx, 1992). Obtainable from the Lynx Educational Trust, PO Box 500, Nottingham NG1 3AS.
3. See James Lindsay, "Bishops Unite to Fight Fur Trade," *Church of England Newspaper*, November 27, 1992.
4. Hugh Montefiore, "Forty-One Against Fur," *Church Times*, January 1, 1992.
5. *Animals and Ethics*, par. 88, p. 38, and *passim*.
6. Montefiore in *The Times*, argued that "I should have thought that, on any showing, we have a prior duty to prevent stress and suffering by domesticated rather than wild animals, since wild species in the course of nature have been subject to predation, while domestic species have not. So I would pay more attention to predominantly urban abolitionists of fox-hunting if they gave priority in their publicity to the stress suffered by millions of hens in batteries rather than the comparatively few foxes in the hunting field." Inconsistently, when faced with a precise issue, namely the stress and inhumane conditions of farmed, fur-bearing wild animals (which

arguably suffer *more* because they have not been so domesticated),
we find Montefiore writing in justification. To those who argue that
we shouldn't be concerned about one species of animal because another may suffer more, there is only one question to be asked: And
what have you done to prevent *their* suffering?

7. John Whale, "Every Moving Thing That Liveth Shall Be Meat for
   You," *Church Times* (editorial), April 8, 1993, p. 10. Among the many
   misjudgments is the claim that the humanitarian movement of the
   eighteenth century and beyond was based on "compassionate
   rather than scriptural grounds." In fact, Christian pioneers of the
   humane treatment of animals made frequent and assiduous reference to Scripture as the true grounds of compassion for animals,
   and none more forcefully than Humphry Primatt, who wrote the
   first seminal text, *The Duty of Mercy and the Sin of Cruelty* in 1776,
   reprinted by Edwin Mellen Press, edited with an introduction by
   Andrew Linzey, 1999.

8. "Canadian Bishop Comes to Seal-Hunters' Aid," *Church Times*, April
   8, 1993, p. 2.

9. Carol McKenna, letter to the *Church Times*, April 23, 1993, p. 11, my
   emphasis. The figures given are for the 1990/1 season. In 1997, the
   number of trapped wild animals worldwide is closer to 30 million–
   35 million so the figures need to be amended accordingly. I am
   grateful to Mark Glover of Respect for Animals for this information
   and for his kind assistance with this chapter.

10. *Defense of the Fur Trade*, A discussion paper prepared by the Depart-
    ment of External Affairs, Canada (May 1985), p. 9. I am grateful to
    Dr. David Lavigne for this reference.

11. Rod Cumberland, Furbearer Biologist with the New Brunswick
    Province, letter, July 13, 1993; original emphasis. The letter further
    acknowledges that non-native trappers "trap 95 per cent of our an-
    imals" and that "most non-native trappers trap as a hobby."

12. The Canadian Standing Committee on Aboriginal Affairs boasted
    that, "In the most recent case, in February 1993, the Church of En-
    gland bishops modified their position on the endorsement of an
    anti-trapping publication. Aboriginal representatives were able to
    demonstrate successfully to the Bishop of London their depen-
    dence on the fur-trade," *Canada Fur Watch: Aboriginal Livelihood at Risk*
    (Fifth Report, SCOAA, May 1993), p. 24. Despite the boast, no
    bishop who was a signatory to the publication has withdrawn his
    name. From the document it appears that natives were given
    "$15,000 for its February European visit" from the Department of In-
    dian Affairs and Northern Development (DIAND) which included
    canvasing the then Bishop of London, p. 25.

13. "Federal Government Invests in Wild Fur Industry," News Release
    Communique (Ottawa: Government of Canada, May 21, 1993), p. 2.

I am grateful to Carol McKenna for this documentation and also for 11 and 12 above.

14. Extract (revised) from Andrew Linzey, "Introduction: The Christian Case Against Cruelty," *Cruelty and Christian Conscience*, p. 16.

15. Ibid, pp. 18–19.

Chapter 15 Works of Darkness, Signs of Light

1. Recently the Bishop of Dorchester, Anthony Russell, warned against the "demonization" of farmers. Russell's pastoral care for the farming community is well-known and should be respected, but he fails to make the distinction between "farmers" and "farming," assuming that criticism of one is always criticism of the other. Indeed, he blames such demonization—at least implicitly—on "powerful conservation and animal rights organizations" which allegedly shape current "attitudes" toward the countryside and farming. Oh that our attitudes were so shaped! It is sad to see a bishop under the guise of (rightly) opposing the demonization of farmers effectively doing the same to conservationists and animal advocates. A more pastorally sensitive bishop might help the present debate by trying to understand the widespread ethical unease about modern farming practices, even by helping farmers to see the explicitly ethical dimension to their work. Needless to say, the welfare of animals is not addressed as an issue in his article, "Putting Our Hand to the Plough," *Church Times*, January 9, 1997, p. 8.

2. *Veritatis Splendor*, p. 121.

3. Seamus Heaney, "The Early Purges," *Death of a Naturalist* [1966] (London: Faber and Faber, 1991), p. 11.

4. This is based on the figure of 7 percent for practicing Roman Catholics and the (surely now conservative) estimate of 10 percent for vegetarians and vegans augmented by the growing number of demi-vegetarians.

5. For an account of the RSPCA's struggle to achieve minimum standards of humane slaughter, see Edward G. Fairholme and Wellesley Pain, *A Century of Work for Animals: The History of the* RSPCA, 1824–1924 (London: John Murray, 1924), chapter XI, pp. 173–90.

6. Born Free Foundation and the World Society for the Protection of Animals, *The Zoo Inquiry* (September 5, 1994), pp. 1–56 (obtainable from the Born Free Foundation, Cherry Tree Cottage, Coldharbour, Dorking, Surrey RH5 6HA). Animal Aid, *A Brutal Business: An Investigation into the Treatment of Animals at Livestock Auctions* (1997), pp. 1–24 (obtainable from Animal Aid, The Old Chapel, Bradford Street, Tonbridge, Kent TN9 1AW).

7. Among the outstanding exposés are: *It's a Dog Life* (on animal experimentation at Huntingdon Life Sciences laboratory) by Small

World Productions, 1a Waterlow Rd, London N19 5NJ; *Fur—the Bloody Choice* (on fur farming) by Respect for Animals, PO Box 500, Nottingham NG1 3AS; *Hens Might Fly* (on hen batteries) by Compassion in World Farming, 5a Charles Street, Petersfield, Hants GU32 3EH; *Paradise Lost* (on the trade in primates for research) by the British Union for the Abolition of Vivisection, 16 Crane Grove, London N7 8LB; *The Zoochotic Report* (on stress suffered by zoo animals) by the Born Free Foundation, address above.

8. For information about their respective educational publications, contact the Education Department, RSPCA, Causeway, Horsham, West Sussex RH12 1HG, and the IFAW Charitable Trust, Pantiles Chambers, 85 High Street, Tunbridge Wells, Kent TN1 1YG.

9. A range of set-text anthologies on animals and ethics (comprising extracts of works both for and against animals) designed for university courses has been published over the last fifteen years, including: Tom Regan and Peter Singer (eds.), *Animal Rights and Human Obligations* (New York: Prentice Hall International, 2nd ed., 1993); Andrew Linzey and Tom Regan (eds.), *Animals and Christianity: A Book of Readings*; P. A. B. Clarke and Andrew Linzey (eds.), *Political Theory and Animal Rights*; and Andrew Linzey and Dorothy Yamamoto (eds.), *Animals on the Agenda*.

10. For details of their pioneering work, contact Beauty Without Cruelty UK Office: 57 King Henry's Walk, London N1 4NH; U.S. Office: 175 W. 12th Street, New York, NY 10011. There is also an excellent educational video on the intelligence and sentience of pigs for sixteen-to-eighteen-year-olds titled *Stimulus Response*, produced by the Association of Animal Behavior, Homerton College, Cambridge CB2 2PH.

11. See their two publications: *Animal Testing: Ending the Pain* (1996) and *The Co-operative Bank: What We Are and What We Stand For* (1992); the latter details their ethical guidelines for investment. For more information, contact The Co-operative Bank, 1 Balloon Street, Manchester M60 4EP.

12. "Freedom Food" promises meat derived from husbandry systems that aim at the "Five Freedoms" for farm animals, including freedom "to express normal behavior," see the leaflet "Help to Improve the Welfare of Britain's 750 Million Farm Animals" (RSPCA, 1997), p. 2.

13. See, for example, the Report of the European Scientific Veterinary Committee, *The Welfare of Intensively Kept Pigs* (September 30, 1997), pp. 1–208, which recommends against tail docking of pigs on welfare grounds, maintaining that tail-biting (the usual argument for docking) is "an indication of an inadequate environment and indicates that welfare is poor in the animal carrying out the biting," p. 60; also recommendation, p. 143.

14. The full frank details are given in Alan Clark, *Diaries* (London: Phoenix, 1994), pp. 214–16.
15. *The Times* (editorial), April 25, 1800; cited in A. W. Moss, *The Valiant Crusade*, p. 14.
16. My article "Towards a Christian Socialist View of Animals" was published in *The Christian Socialist*, Journal of the CSM, in 1971.
17. MORI Opinion Poll on Animal Welfare, *Daily Telegraph*.

Chapter 16   Christ-like Ministry to Other Creatures

1. *Daily Telegraph* (editorial), January 10, 1995, p. 18.
2. Malcolm Muggeridge, *Chronicles of Wasted Time*, vol. 1. *The Green Stick* (London: Collins, 1972), p. 123.
3. Psalm 24:1.
4. Andrew Linzey, *Animal Rites: Liturgies of Animal Care* (London: SCM Press, 1999); distributed in the United States by Trinity Press International.
5. Andrew Linzey, *An Order of Service for Animal Welfare and/or Blessing* (Horsham: RSPCA, 1975), pp. 1–17; available from the Education Department of the RSPCA.
6. "Anti-bat campaigners, led by Catherine Ward, who complained about bats in churches of her husband's benefice in Norfolk, have launched the Movement Against Bats in Churches (Mabic)," *Church Times*, October 9, 1992, p. 1. For details of the bizarre correspondence see the *Church Times*, August 21 and 28, September 11 and October 16. The legislation concerned is the *Wildlife and Countryside Act* 1981 which provides basic safeguards for endangered species.
7. Dr. J. Cuthbert, a biologist, who advises local authorities on pigeons, writes, "Despite statements to the contrary, pigeon droppings are in fact chemically incapable of corroding building materials. Pigeons and their droppings are also no more hazardous to human health than any other animal species and are safer than most. Given these facts, it is not clear why pigeons should not be tolerated on churches, cathedrals and other religious buildings, and valued for their grace and interesting ways. However, should pigeons not be wanted on buildings, there are various effective measures to deter their presence or to remove their reasons for perching at particular locations. Perching deterrents which are effective and which do not trap or injure birds include spikes (which are available in various colors and can be simply glued on to building surfaces) and tipplers. Spikes can be relatively inexpensive, depending on the supplier. Antiperching gel should not be used: it can be lethal to birds, can damage buildings and has a short effectiveness time. Due to deterioration with time or defective installation, nets have to be checked regularly to release trapped birds.

Culling is a waste of time and money: pigeon numbers simply re-
generate. There are also no humane ways of culling feral pigeons."
For more information contact, Dr. J. Cuthbert, Brookside Cottage,
Glovers Road, Charlwood, Surrey RH6 0EG. For details of the non-
lethal nest box control of pigeons, contact The B C Group Trust, PO
Box 102, Newmarket, Suffolk CB8 0RU.

8. Mark Roskill (ed.), *The Letters of Van Gogh* [1927–29] (London:
Fontana, 1982), p. 124.

9. The Bishop of London, Richard Chartres, cited in *Church of England
Newspaper*, June 6, 1997, p. 1. Sadly, a review of the original interview
in *Time for a Change* (June/July, 1995) indicates that the reported remarks were accurate.

10. Colossians 1:19f.

11. *Animal Theology*, p. 124.

12. Romans 8:18–24.

13. Donald Coggan, RSPCA *Today*.

14. John 10:12.

15. Stephen Pattinson, *Pastoral Care and Liberation Theology* (London:
SPCK, 1994).

16. Richard Bauckham, *The Bible in Politics: How to Read the Bible Politically*
(London: SPCK, 1989), p. 47, original emphasis.

17. See II Enoch (the Slavonic Apolcalypse of Enoch), chapters 58–59;
cited and discussed in Richard Bauckham, "Jesus and the Animals
I: What Did He Teach?" in *Animals on the Agenda*, pp. 34–35. The
theme is also developed in Axel Munthe, *The Story of San Michele*
(London: John Murray, 1948).

18. Henry Vaughan, from "The Book" in *Silex Scintillans* (1655), extract in
Compassion for Animals: Readings and Prayers, p. 87, and in Stephen
R. L. Clark, *The Moral Status of Animals* (Oxford: Oxford University
Press), inside page.

Printed in the United Kingdom
by Lightning Source UK Ltd.
116511UKS00001B/310-327